IT Demystified

The IT handbook for business professionals

First edition (revised)

Ade McCormack

AURIDIAN

Published by Auridian Press
PO Box 733
Great Missenden HP16 9QJ UK

Tel: +44 (0) 1494 866 799
www.auridian.com

First published in Great Britain in 2004. Issue 7.3
© Adrian Gerald McCormack 2008

ISBN 0-9547651-0-9

British Library Cataloguing in Publication Data
A CIP catalogue record for this book can be obtained from the British Library

Whilst reasonable effort has been taken to ensure the veracity of the information contained in this book, Auridian and the author take no responsibility for any negative consequences arising from the application of the contents of this book.

Auridian's policy is to use paper manufactured from sustainable forests.

Auridian Press is a division of Auridian Consulting Ltd.

In praise of IT Demystified

"Even those of us who spend our working lives writing about IT can get confused by the jargon to which the industry seems addicted. Ade McCormack uses humour and sharp observation to steer the reader through the alphabet soup of acronyms and buzzwords, enabling them to gain a real understanding of what IT means in the 21st-century enterprise."

Andrew Baxter, Former Editor
Financial Times – IT Review

Most directors would probably admit that IT is a mystery to them. Yet business leaders are what this book calls "IT influencers", needing the right technology to drive cost out of the business and compete in new or existing markets.

McCormack's book succeeds in making the IT framework of business understandable to the most hopeless technophobe. Based on a seminar run by his consulting firm, it takes the reader painlessly from the basic building blocks of the PC, through the systems that drive a company, to anticipating tomorrow's hot developments.

Along the way it explains all that tiresome trade jargon with a nice leavening of humour. At nearly £30, this sturdy paperback may seem expensive, but it will repay its cost many times over in producing informed IT decisions

Director Magazine – Toolbox Review – Rated '5 spanners'
Institute of Directors

"IT Demystified has been long awaited. It relates in simple language what all professionals should know about technology. From the very first page it explains jargon and technology in a way that any executive can understand. A must for every senior executive."

Phil Garvey, Chairman, IT in the Boardroom
Intellect

"'IT Demystified' by Ade McCormack is the must have technology thesaurus for any of us attempting survival in today's commercial world. Excellent as an executive toy for reference purposes, but also a surprisingly good commuting read due to its concise and often witty prose."

Ann Swain, Chief Executive
Association of Technology Staffing Companies

"In IT Demystified Ade has gone a long way, in his engaging style, to dispel the myths and complexities that can make IT so daunting. It is an essential read for every manager; for those of us who have a suspicion that use of technology will help our business but don't know where to start, and for those of us who are in the industry and think we know or should know, but don't feel able to ask!"

Terry Watts, Chief Operating Officer
eSkills UK

"A wonderful tool for HR Professionals working in this field. We can now speak the same language with our internal customers!"

Satty Kenth, HR Manager - UK, Ireland, Benelux & Germany
Electrolux IT

Acknowledgements

I would like to thank everyone involved in the IT industry for making it such an interesting sector to work in over the last few decades. I am blessed with parents who did not feel obliged to prescribe a career for me. Consequently my passion for IT and its impact on business remains undiminished to this day.

I would like to thank my wife Adèle for her loving support to me. Despite my presence she manages to make our home an oasis of tranquillity. I would also like to thank my son Matthew for reminding me of life's priorities. Though I feel his approach of climbing onto my desk and attempting to unscrew my head is a little harsh. He's 5 years old. Despite his first words sounding remarkably like 'visual basic', which as you can imagine brought a tear to my eye, I suspect he is destined for a career in Greco-Roman wrestling.

Contents at a Glance

Contents

Chapter 0

Introduction

Why read this book?

IT departments, and to a large extent the IT Sector in general, have done very little to make IT understandable to the user community. They have inadvertently or otherwise created their own exclusive language, which serves to ensure that non-IT people know their place in the grand technology pecking order.

In fairness, the user experience has improved measurably over the last few decades. The more intuitive graphical user interfaces of modern PCs along with the standardisation of the 'look and feel' of desktop applications attests to this. However the same cannot be said in terms of the opaque language that has evolved from the marketing departments of technology companies.

You are an IT influencer

There are a great many people who are more than just users. Their role, whilst business focused, has a significant IT element. Such people are what I call IT influencers.

This book is aimed at IT influencers. Such people typically need to:

- ❑ Use IT to create or improve (read today as 'drive cost out of') one or more business processes. ie automate.
- ❑ Use IT to gain competitive advantage through leveraging what the organization knows about itself and its markets. Ie. informate.

- Sell IT related services to end user organizations, eg. recruitment consultants, software solution providers, outsourcers
- Provide a credible support function to the IT department, eg. the HR department.

To be an influencer you need to have credibility. To be credible in the IT arena you need to 'speak the language', understand the trends and be conscious of the associated issues and opportunities.

What this book will do for you

IT Demystified will do all of this for you. It differs from other attempts at this subject matter in a number of very important ways:

- It is very commercially focused. This is not a university text book, unless your university is interested in grooming its IT and business undergraduates for the real world
- It avoids technicalities unless such detail will significantly enhance your credibility in respect of influencing IT matters
- It will give you the big picture. You will have a strong sense of how the main pieces of the IT jigsaw fit together
- It is tried and tested. This book is based on Auridian Consulting's IT Demystified seminar, which since 1996 has been delivered to many thousands of business influencers.

How does it feel?

My experience in dealing with this subject enables me to understand the emotions you may well be feeling at this moment. Let me guess, does one of the following apply to you?

a. "IT is what IT people do. I don't really want to know. I've got this far in life by wearing my 'technophobe colours' with pride"

b. "The very word IT conjures up childhood trauma. IT sits along with maths, physics and chemistry in terms of its ability to make me squirm"

c. "I am smart enough to recognise that influencing IT-related business matters is the new 21st century competency. If I don't embrace that fact, I'll be replaced by someone that does."

Type 'a's are unlikely to buy this book of their own accord. So if you are a type 'a' you are either in the midst of an organizational culture change, and reading this book has been deemed in your best interest by someone else, or you have simply picked up the wrong book.

Type 'b's fret not. This book is called IT Demystified because that is what it will do. I have worked with people whose experience of being an IT influencer can only sound impressive when expressed in minutes! I am pleased to say such people have gone on to be very effective IT influencers.

Type 'c's, you are ahead of the curve. You have recognised that the IT/e-business steamroller is picking up speed and you have decided to drive it rather than become 'e-road kill'.

About the Author

I graduated from Leicester University with an honours degree in Physics with Astrophysics, and with my childhood love of Astronomy completely shredded. No fault of the University, I just thought we would learn the names of all the planets and watch the occasional meteor shower. Course work that included cosmology, statistical thermodynamics and quantum physics gave me a yearning for a simpler world.

My final year project (thesis to the easily impressed) to search for black holes by trawling digital observational data captured across two separate wavelengths had a very high computing component. The simplicity of 'ones and zeros' proved irresistible to me. From that point on I knew that my space aspirations were grounded.

Thus I applied to a number of computer firms. Not knowing whether my computing experience had value in the commercial world I pursued any line of opportunity that would get me in. In my quest I got a response back from a company called Ferranti Computer Systems informing me that I would be unsuitable for the post of technical author, but would I like to come along and be interviewed for the role of programmer. So for the next three years I designed and developed real-time naval command and control software systems.

I then spent 7 years at Logica (now LogicaCMG) working in a variety of technical and technical management roles. I had the opportunity to work with Credit Suisse First Boston, Admiralty Surface Weapons Establishment, Royal Navy, Marconi, The European Space Agency (my degree did have some use) and the Coastguard Agency.

My experiences working at the sharp end of IT highlighted the void that existed between IT people and non-IT people. I thus set about bridging this gap by forming Auridian Consulting. Since January 1996, Auridian has worked with hundreds of end-user and technology companies. This has given me the opportunity to work with a variety of organizations, big and small across the world. My activities include training, coaching, public speaking, consulting and content provision.

I pay very close attention to the Technology Sector. Both blue chip organizations and the media seek my views. I have an opinion column in the Financial Times and am editorial adviser to a number of publications including MIS (targeting IT leadership) and IT training (targeting IT training organizations/specialists). You might find my Tech Sector Review newsletter a time efficient approach to keeping up with the market – **www.auridian.com/tsr.**

Please note that my attempts at humour/satire throughout the book are in fact:

- ❑ Grounded in market realities
- ❑ Designed to lighten what for some might be a dry subject
- ❑ ~~Funny.~~

How to use this book

'Knowledge is power' is a recurrent theme in respect of the IT arena. There are a lot of knowledgeable people around who don't seem to be getting anywhere in life. I think the winning philosophy is 'Applied knowledge is power'. Weaving information into conversations and written communications is key to being an IT influencer. Thus it is not enough to read this book and understand it. You will start to make an impact when you demonstrate your understanding to those you need to influence.

Wise up

Many would-be IT influencers do not have the confidence to engage in technology related conversations. This sends out 'I'm a fraud'/'I don't deserve to be here' type signals when the subject of IT crops up. Those 'more in the know' can smell this in much the same way as sharks can smell blood and dogs can smell fear. Thus the key skill is taking such people 'off the scent' by throwing in a few sage comments at key stages of the conversation (Think primacy and recency effects, which refer to the importance of making a positive impression on initial and final contact with someone).

So impressive IT influencers not only understand IT, albeit an inch deep but a mile wide, but they know how to let others know they know. This book is designed to help you make a positive impression. The terms are explained in sound bites so that you can easily weave them into your conversation. You hear the word Java, you interject "Why is having a bandwidth friendly platform independent object oriented programming language important to you?" This may be over the top, but it will make people tread more respectfully when they talk to you about IT.

Introduction

Book structure

Think of this book as your survival kit in the IT jungle. It is divided into sections as follows:

Section	In essence
1	The key elements of IT
2	Programming languages and databases
3	IT system blueprints
4	The IT Department
5	New technologies

- Book structure

Section 1 - The Fundamental Framework
The building blocks of IT

This covers the IT basics. Hardware, software and data are explained, as are more advanced concepts such as operating systems and applications, including enterprise applications.

- ❑ Chapter 1 – IT basics
- ❑ Chapter 2 – Hardware
- ❑ Chapter 3 – Operating systems
- ❑ Chapter 4 – Application software

Section 2 - Application development

The importance of programming languages and databases

Why applications are so important to business and how they are built are covered here.

❑ Chapter 5 – Application development

Section 3 - Architectures

How IT systems hang together

Here we see how technology has evolved from the original mainframes and dumb terminals right through to what we have today and beyond. In effect we are covering IT architectures.

❑ Chapter 6 – Carbon dating the IT investment

❑ Chapter 7 – 21st century systems

Section 4 - Within the IT department

What happens 'over the fence'

This section examines the structure of an IT department, along with how systems are built.

❑ Chapter 8 – The IT department

❑ Chapter 9 – How IT systems are built

Section 5 - New Technologies

What's hot today and what will be hot tomorrow

The Internet, World Wide Wait (sorry Web) and e-business are covered here, along with what to expect in the foreseeable.

❑ Chapter 10 –What's hot today

❑ Chapter 11 –What's hot tomorrow

Introduction

The book is riddled with what might look like asides, or irrelevant information. Whilst delivered in a light perhaps even frivolous tone, these are essentially insights into the friction that exists between the IT and business communities. The more experienced you are as an IT influencer the more you will appreciate these asides.

The book also concentrates on IT from an organizational perspective rather than a home user perspective. Many people happily use their computing systems (ie their PC) to idly surf the web or play computer games. These are equally valid uses of IT, though the IT department are very likely to take a different view if these activities are carried out using company resources.

I discovered the hard way that IT is a lot easier than astrophysics. After reading this book you will find that IT is not the migraine-inducing subject that it appears to be. Who knows, you may even feel the urge to rush out and buy an anorak!

Ade McCormack
Auridian
ade@auridian.com
www.auridian.com/ade

Section 1

The Fundamental Framework
The building blocks of IT

This covers the IT basics. Hardware, software and data are explained, as are more advanced concepts such as operating systems and applications, including enterprise applications.

- ❑ Chapter 1 – IT basics
- ❑ Chapter 2 – Hardware
- ❑ Chapter 3 – Operating systems
- ❑ Chapter 4 – Application software

Chapter 1

IT Basics

Why read this? This chapter lays out the rationale behind IT systems in business and their main components.

Easy does it!

Let's start very gently. First I'll answer a few fundamental questions so that you can get some learning foundations in place.

What is the point of IT?

Sadly this question is often asked at Board level in many businesses. It perhaps reflects a technophobic attitude and/or a perception that the IT department is not delivering good value for money.

Having got that off my chest, let's press on.

To automate

The first use of IT was to *automate* processes that were carried out manually or mechanically. Thus the original focus of IT was on automation. Examples include:

- Factory automation - picture the robotic arm lowering down onto the car factory production line
  - Good system – Pick up the car and paint it, pick up the car and paint it, pick up......
  - Bad system - Smash the car, paint the air, smash the car, paint the air...
  - Such systems need to be very finely tuned!
- Bank statement production

Less human involvement generally means less error.

Whilst using IT for automation is to some extent seen as 'old hat', the drive to automate business processes is spreading across the planet like a forest fire as companies race to drive costs (and often people) out of their business processes.

To informate

So initially computers were used to automate. A perhaps more valuable use of IT is to *informate*. Organizations have built up large repositories of data, relating to their internal activities and to what they know about the markets they operate in.

The challenge is to harness this data, which is usually spread almost randomly across the business, in such a manner that business users can make critical business decisions. Today such users are referred to as knowledge workers.

Thus IT is helping organizations to use the data they own to make smarter and perhaps quicker business decisions. Examples include:

- Retail stores deciding which customers to invite to their private shopping evening

❑ Whether the rate of decrease in the number of outstanding defects on a 'soon to be released' product necessitates a delay in the launch.

Technology architectures (more of this in section 3) enable data generated by users to be shared within the organization. This enhances the decision making process.

The informating aspects of IT are very much in vogue today, with a strong leaning towards customer/market-focused intelligence.

So in a nutshell IT exists to either automate or informate.

What is an IT system?

In essence it is a collection of technologies that enables an organization to:
- ❑ Automate certain activities
  - o For example letter writing
- ❑ Informate certain activities
  - o For example detecting customer-buying patterns.

To answer this question in a more dry and technically focused manner, an IT system comprises a collection of hardware and software components that enable an organization to carry out one or more business functions.

For a home user, their IT system may just be a PC running a word processor. For a multinational organization, their IT system may comprise many computers linked together across the planet.

How do IT systems work?

It's really quite simple. If we think of an IT system as a 'black box', actually it could be a 'white box', the point is that you can't see inside it and aren't particularly interested in what is inside it. Think of this box as representing the IT system.

Essentially the role of this box is to convert data into information. That is to say:

- The data is put into the system (input)
- The box cleverly processes the data
- When the users need to access the system useful information comes out (output).

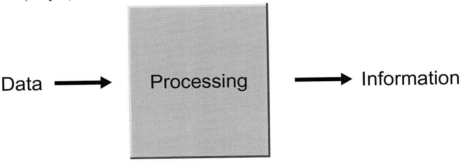

1.1 An IT system

So for example employee records are added to the IT system and at some point in the future a user wants to know how many people are due to retire in the next three months. So it could be said that data, for example a stack of resumes, is not particularly useful, but information, ie. a specific query related to that data is of use. So one of the key roles of the computer is to convert data into information.

This begs the question so how does the transformation of data to information take place. Well that is where software comes into play. The role of (application) software is to primarily convert data into information. More generally software is the stuff that makes the hardware do things. Without software your computer would be merely an inefficient yet expensive room heater.

Administrative systems

The example I have given here is of what might be called an administrative or databased system. These systems usually take their input directly from a user or from another system. Information is obtained from the system as and when needed.

Real-time systems

The alternative type of system is known as a real-time system. Such systems respond instantly to an external stimulus. To fail to do so could have a catastrophic impact on the user/user's organization. The IT systems embedded within modern cars are designed to operate in real-time. Consequently your brakes respond at the time you apply them, rather than at some point in the future. Typically real-time systems are always 'on guard' awaiting input, which can come from a user (applying the brakes) or an external stimulus (the temperature drops below $17°$ centigrade, so causing the air conditioning heater to kick in).

Ten years ago the only people interested in real-time systems would have been the military or those involved in some form of process control (eg. car manufacturing). Today we all encounter real-time systems. Examples include:

- Mobile phones
- Cars
- Air conditioning
- Financial data feeds.

In summary IT systems use software, which runs on hardware to convert data into information. In some cases this information may give rise to an action, for example the application of the brakes to the wheels of your car.

What are the key elements of an IT system?

We have already mentioned that IT systems are made up of hardware and software. That's really it.

If the IT system is for a single user then the hardware will most likely be a PC or an Apple iMac, or even a Palm Treo. However if the system is for multiple users then it is most likely that these user devices will be connected to larger computers that serve up, or simply provide, access to shared resources such as email, files, databases and even the web.

Such computers are for this reason known as servers. User devices and servers are linked to each other using network technology, which in its simplest form is just metal cabling. However advances in networking technology have added wireless and fibre optic cabling to the options we have when linking computers together.

It is worth highlighting that the clever bit of IT is the software. Software turns your PC into a word processor, games console, web browser or even a radio. The hardware simply provides the medium to enable software to do what it does. Thus the smart technology companies are migrating their offerings away from hardware and into software. Technology companies that do not take this onboard are in varying stages of terminal decline.

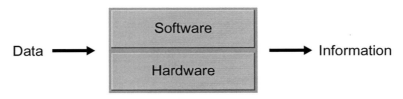

1.2 Elements of an IT system

The Fundamental Framework

We have mentioned hardware and software and their relation to each other. We will now explore these in a little more detail. Figure 1-3 reveals a number of interesting facts:

❑ Software is split into two layers, the operating system and application software.

❑ The operating system plus the hardware are often referred to as the platform.

1-3 The Fundamental Framework

We will explore all of this in more detail in the remaining chapters in this section. But it is worth saying at this stage that operating system software makes the computer *usable*, but application software makes the computer *useful*. Consequently users only care about application software. This is the stuff that helps them do their work, quicker, better, more profitably. But application software needs a platform to run on, thus the IT department is focused on all three layers of the fundamental framework.

Please note that all computers have these three layers, from the tiniest palmtop to the largest super server. This diagram already applies to the very latest mobile phones. It will eventually apply to your television, fridge and bathroom cabinet. It is thus a diagram worth remembering.

To complete the picture one really needs to take the networking side into account. Again the cleverness in networking actually resides in the computers and not the cable. This functionality is built into the operating system and the card installed on the computer that connects it to the network.

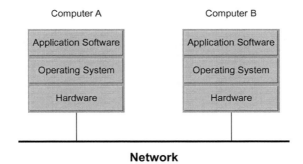

1.4 Networked computers

Front and back-end

At this point it is also worth mentioning that IT systems can be subdivided into front-end and back-end. In short, front-end is the technology (both hardware and software) that the user directly uses and the back-end is the technology that the user indirectly uses (via the front-end technology). Servers are an example of back-end technology. In a large organization these will be housed within the perimeter of the IT department. In a smaller organization it is possible to find the server hidden under cloths and dustpans in the broom cupboard. A whirring staircase is a dead giveaway.

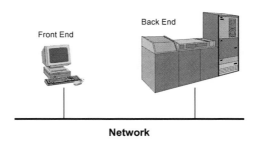

1.5 Front-end and back-end

The remaining chapters in this section focus on the three layers of the fundamental framework.

In summary

- ❑ Businesses use IT systems to either automate processes and/or gain competitive advantage through using their data to anticipate trends
- ❑ IT systems essentially convert data into information. Software makes this transformation possible
- ❑ Software needs hardware to function
- ❑ Software can be classified into operating system and application software.

Test yourself?

1. Businesses use IT systems to:
   a. Impress clients
   b. Automate business processes
   c. Make key decisions
   d. Keep their IT staff employed.
2. A typical business user:
   a. Has very strong views on the choice of operating system
   b. Has relatively strong views on the colour of the hardware
   c. Only cares about the productivity enhancements delivered by the applications
   d. Are fascinated by the possibilities that may arise from the introduction of an integrated thin-client, utility based, heterogeneous web services architecture.

3. Software:
   a. Provides a platform from which to run the hardware
   b. Is just the aspects of hardware that are not hard, eg. the mouse pad
   c. Is where the real value of an IT system resides
   d. Is another name for a computer program.
4. The fundamental framework:
   a. Only relates to servers
   b. Is made up of hardware and software
   c. Requires the applications to be in place before the operating system will run
   d. Oracle is the number one fundamental framework supplier.

Chapter 2

Hardware

Why read this? This chapter focuses on the hardware layer of the fundamental framework. Without hardware there would be no IT industry. Thus it is a critical to understanding IT.

What is hardware?

Hardware is conceptually (and physically) easy to grasp. It is:

- ❑ Tangible
- ❑ Makes a whirring noise
- ❑ Hurts (to varying degrees) if you drop it on your big toe.

Neither hardware vendors nor health experts recommend this test.

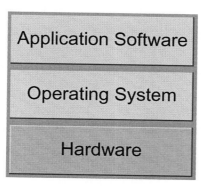

2.1 Hardware

It is usually beige in colour, but fashion-conscious technology suppliers, such as Apple, have broken rank. They offer a beautiful range of pastel shades for those whose key functional requirement is to ensure the desktop matches the Venetian blinds in their split-level minimalist apartment.

Peripherals

Hardware is not restricted to computers. It also embraces peripherals, which are the bits one can attach directly or indirectly to your computer. Examples include printers, plotters, disk drives, scanners, joy sticks and even credit card readers. NB. Some of these peripherals have become so sophisticated that they can be added directly to the network and behave as if they are computers in their own right. Examples include network-attached printers and network-attached storage (often referred to as NAS).

Front-end

The PC is currently the most common example of a front-end computer. Other examples of front-end technology include:

- ❑ Smart phones
- ❑ Palmtops (aka PDAs – Personal Digital Assistants)
- ❑ Laptops
- ❑ Carpettops
  - o The TV is slowly evolving into a web access device.

We should clarify what a PC is. Some might say 'personal computer'. Before IBM arrived on the desktop scene that is indeed what it stood for. Thus an Apple Mac was a PC, as was a Commodore 64, Atari 400 and Sinclair ZX80.

But IBM caused a seismic shift in the world of computing when it redefined the PC as a desktop computer based on a processing chip created by a little known company called Intel, and ran an operating system licensed (not created) by an upstart company called Microsoft. Both Intel and Microsoft owe a lot to IBM, which accelerated the growth of the 'PC' market by making its specification freely available to those that wanted to copy it. So similarly companies such as Dell and Gateway owe a lot to IBM.

The net effect is that all other PCs are a sideshow to the IBM PC architecture. A word of warning, some Apple users may have a view on this.

2.2 Front-end technology

But what about Apple?

Apple users come in two categories:

- ❑ Zealot – 'How dare you show disrespect to the greatest piece of user friendly technology known to mankind'
- ❑ Ultra trendy – ' Well I haven't actually ever used it, but doesn't it look cool in my split-level ….'.

The latter are harmless and just overly susceptible to life style based marketing. The former are happy to fight to the death over their Apple conviction. They have a point; it just so happens that it gets smaller on a daily basis as Apple technology becomes marginalized from a commercial computing perspective. Please note that Apple is actively addressing this.

Back-end

The generic term for the computer at the back-end (ie. out of sight of the users) is known as a server. But you may also hear the term mainframe, mid-range and even minicomputer. In short mainframe and minicomputers are technology from a bygone era. Mainframes are still in use, but they are something of a career cul-de-sac for IT specialists. Mid range computers were a slightly more modern version of a mainframe designed to service hundreds rather than thousands of users. Mini computers are few and far between. More on mainframes in chapter 6.

This may sound as if back-end computing is lagging technologically behind its front-end cousins. Not so. Mainframes and mid ranges computers are still rolling off the conveyor belt, it's just that they are referred to as servers. Those at the top end of the server range are often referred to as high-end or super servers.

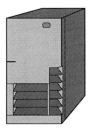

2.3 Back-end technology

Blade Server

In fact a new development in server technology, the blade server, enables IT departments to, in effect, add another server to their set-up just by sliding a tray-like 'processor board' into what looks like a very large toast rack. Only a few years ago these blade servers would have had the volume of a washing machine.

Moore's Law

This brings to mind what is known as Moore's Law. Gordon Moore was a founder of Intel who back in 1965 predicted that chip capacity (ie. processing power) would double every year. In latter years this has slowed down, and so the law has been modified to double capacity every 18 months. Nonetheless this still represents very impressive growth.

A commodity

Back-end server technology has become more or less a commodity market. Vendors are locked into a vicious circle (for them) of expensive innovation coupled with free-falling pricing. However server hardware is a useful tool in cementing a relationship with a client. Once purchased the client has in many cases 'locked' themselves into the vendor. The vendor can now offer more value-added services that complement the server hardware, which in turn locks the client in deeper. After a short period the client could not drop the vendor without severe disruption to their IT infrastructure. So whilst not a high margin business, servers are a key element in the client 'relationship' toolkit.

Tailored versus 'off the shelf'

In building IT systems, every effort is made to use standardised hardware. The PC is a good example of this. However not all IT systems are built to run in cosy air-conditioned offices. Alternative environments include:

- Within cars
  - Car management systems
- In deserts
  - Oil-well or military scenarios
- In supermarkets
  - Stock management or point of sale devices.

Ruggedised

Sometimes the hardware may look like office hardware, but is simply ruggedised. PCs on a war ship are ruggedised to cope with stormy weather and torpedo attacks. The degree of ruggedisation depends on the scenario. So does the PC need to function when a torpedo hits the PC or just when a torpedo hits the hull of the ship? This has all sorts of implications, not least cost.

Tailored

The traditional PC interface of monitor and keyboard is not always the most efficient way to utilize the technology.

Thus the hardware needs to be tailored to the needs of the user. Examples include:

- ❑ ATMs
  - o Aka cash point machines or beer token dispensers
- ❑ Check-out point-of-sale devices
- ❑ Air traffic control systems.

Embedded

IT systems can find themselves embedded within larger systems. Such larger systems include:

- ❑ Mobile phone
- ❑ Car
- ❑ Satellite
- ❑ Nuclear power station

Unsurprisingly opening up a car will not reveal a miniature PC welded onto the car's infrastructure. Embedded systems are more likely to look like a circuit board covered in dust resistant epoxy resin. The fact that the user will access the computer indirectly (via the steering wheel, brakes etc) means that the embedded computer does not need to have its own monitor or a keyboard. It is no less of a computer for this.

Embedded computers need to be tailored to the environment in which they will be used.

Again, wherever possible standard technology is used, because the cost of tailoring hardware is high. As we have seen, certain IT systems need to have an optimised interface and thus tailoring is required.

In summary

- ❏ Hardware is a necessary component of an IT system
- ❏ Most IT systems are based on standard hardware components
- ❏ Users interact with IT via front-end hardware
- ❏ Shared services and resources are provided via the server.

Test yourself?

5. Examples of back-end hardware include:
   a. Mainframes
   b. Servers
   c. Sony PS2
   d. Scanner
6. Examples of front-end hardware include:
   a. A calculator
   b. Commodore64
   c. Mobile phone
   d. Television set.
7. Reasons for having customised hardware include:
   a. Improving the user experience
   b. The need for it to function in a 'non-standard' environment
   c. Making a strong 'fashion statement' to rivals
   d. Being the victim of unscrupulous hardware vendors.
8. Which of the following would register most on the 'foot drop' test:
   a. Palm Pilot
   b. Blade server
   c. PC, with a full hard disk
   d. A mainframe.

Chapter 3

Operating Systems

Why read this? This chapter explains why operating systems exist, which ones are the most popular and the associated market dynamics. They underpin all IT systems and so underpin many IT related discussions. Being lightweight in understanding operating systems will undermine your contribution to the discussion.

Software in general

Before we look at operating systems, it is worth understanding software in general. To recap, software is the stuff that makes the hardware do things. Unlike hardware it is not tangible and so is a little trickier to understand.

Organ grinding

Picture this - Wandering through the narrow streets of Amsterdam you encounter an organ-grinder (for those that have never been to Amsterdam, and even perhaps for those that have, this is a musical instrument) on the corner. You will notice that the revolving barrel determines the tune played by the barrel organ. That barrel can be thought of as the software, which drives the organ (the hardware) to play a particular tune. Changing the barrel changes the tune.

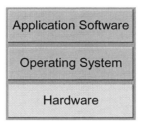

3.1 Software

In this particular example the nodules on the barrel's surface determine the tune. These nodules can be thought of as the specific instructions that determine which note is played. And so it is with software, which is also known as the computer programme. It is essentially a series of instructions that makes the computer behave in a particular manner.

Reliability

Because software is more easily modified than hardware, much of the cleverness built into an IT system is delivered via the software. Similarly this ease of modification has in general given rise to a sloppier attitude to software engineering when compared to hardware engineering. Consequently hardware is generally much more reliable than software.

Digital technology

Software cannot be seen as such. In essence the software that resides on your computer is a collection of ones and zeros. Computers only understand binary. Another name for binary is digital. Hence computers are often referred to as digital technology, as opposed to an old TV or cassette recorder, which are often referred to as analogue technology.

Software storage and execution

The software is stored on computers as files (often with the filename suffixed with .exe – short for executable) on what is known as the hard disk. If you endeavoured to open one of these files in a word processor you would see random characters as the word processor tries to interpret the binary. So don't bother.

Similarly software can be stored on CD-ROMs, diskettes, tape or any other form of media. When the user needs to run the software it is loaded up into what is known as the computer's memory. Each line of the software is executed in turn, thus giving rise to the computer behaving in a particular manner.

Operating Systems

What are they?

Two key points:

- ❑ Operating systems are software
- ❑ Operating systems make the computer usable, but not useful.

Point 1 is important because you will hear people talk about Windows platforms and Unix boxes, which sound very hardware like. What they mean is the hardware in question is running a particular operating system, in this case one from the Windows and Unix family respectively. Be warned, in gardening circles, a Window box is considered to be low-tech.

Point 2 is related to point 1. The operating system is not per se useful, at least not to corporate users. It is the application software that is useful (more on this later). The operating system merely provides the environment that enables the useful stuff (ie the application software) to run.

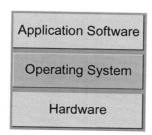

3.2 Operating system

What do they do?

Specifically operating systems give us the following functionality:

- File management –Opening and closing files
  - o Plus directory management
- Memory management – Enabling more than one application to run at the same time
- Peripheral management – Such as printers and scanners
- Multi-tasking - Enabling you to run more than one application on your desktop
- Concurrency – The ability to enable more than one user to access the same computer at the same time
  - o Essential for servers
- Security – To varying degrees
- The look and feel of the user interface
  - o GUI – Graphical User Interface – Comes as standard today.
  - o CUI – Character User Interface – Think 'green screen'.
    - Often light green text on a dark green background.

In 'ancient times' the functionality provided by today's operating systems had to be built into the applications. Separating out the basic common functions from the application specific functions was a major step forward in the world of computing.

Operating systems and standards

Proprietary versus open

There are many operating systems out there, but thankfully they can be categorised as per Diagram 3.3. At this point I need to introduce a couple of pivotal concepts in the world of commercial computing. I present to you the terms 'open' and 'proprietary', two poles in the magnetosphere of IT.

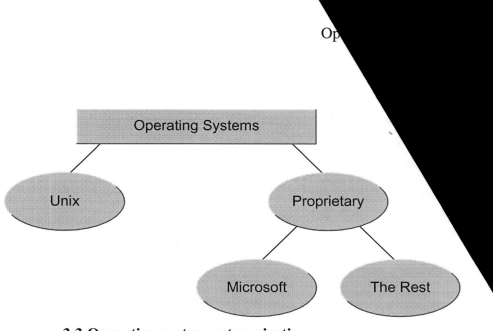

3.3 Operating system categorisation

In this context:

- ❑ Proprietary means under the control of a single vendor
- ❑ Open means the opposite, ie. not under the control of a single vendor.

Ultimately all technologies sold in the market are under the control of the vendor that sells them. But the standards on which their products are based may or may not be under their control.

Microsoft and standards

This is best demonstrated by observing the market. MS Windows, which we will look at in more detail shortly, is under the control of Microsoft. They invented it. Well sort of, they copied it from Apple…who incidentally copied it from Xerox. And they call Xerox the copier company.

Anyway, Microsoft claims that MS Windows is based on standards. It is indeed. Only they are standards created by and controlled by Microsoft. If Mr Bill Gates, founder of Microsoft, wakes up one morning and gets out of bed the wrong side, he may, just because he is in a bad mood, say "I've had it with Windows, we're pulling out of the operating systems business".

If that should happen then it would have a seismic effect on the world of business and thus the world in general. The point here is that he could and no

‾eholder). Thus he runs a dictatorship,
benign dictatorship.

…ᴜed for this. He has achieved business
…ᴋe the power he wields, but we need his
 . this and more importantly pay up. NB. Market
…ₒ dictatorship whilst not in crisis is starting to look

 ᵧou have read so far, would you say that MS Windows is
 ᵧ or open?

Unix and Standards

If that last question proved too challenging, we will now (having just looked at an example of proprietary standards!!) take a look at an example of open standards. Unix, which we will cover in more detail shortly, is based on an international standard that is controlled by a standards body called The Open Group. It is not under the control of just one vendor. But many vendors have created their own versions of Unix based on this standard. Thus there are 'variants' of Unix in the marketplace.

Buyer beware

The vendors of Unix have adhered to the Unix standard, but cheekily have added extra functionality, so that they are in reality selling 'Unix plus'. So they can say that they adhere to the Unix specification, whilst adding very proprietary extensions (thus achieving vendor lock-in by stealth).

This unsatisfactory situation whereby there are different strains of Unix in the marketplace has arisen from the unassertive manner of the associated standards body in promoting just one vendor-neutral version of Unix.

If vendors attempted to omit or modify aspects of Unix defined by the standard, then they would lose the right to brand their operating system as Unix conformant. Thus open standards to some extent keep the vendors under control, but perhaps more importantly (in theory anyway) gives the customer options and alternatives should a vendor relationship be less than satisfactory.

There was a big push towards 'open systems' in the early nineties. Most people mistook this as a push towards using Unix, when in fact it was a push towards open standards in all aspects of computing. For a number of reasons, a truly open system, ie an IT system based purely on open standards, exists only in the 'more pleasant' dreams of IT directors. In summary and in practice, pure proprietary is bad, and pure open is fantasy.

Standards – In summary

But let us get back to the operating systems marketplace. Broadly speaking the title fight in the marketplace is between the Microsoft Windows family and the Unix family. The other proprietary operating systems, whilst in some cases were leaders in their time, are now no more than bit players or just references on the CVs of worldly (sadly read by many as geriatric) information technologists.

Unix

A bit of history

US telecoms giant (at the time) AT&T created Unix in 1969 as a hardware independent operating system. Incidentally it was written in the C programming language, which is still very popular, but more on that later. (Some people find that interesting.)

AT&T for reasons best known to itself gave Unix away to a number of US universities. They in turn evolved it in a number of different directions. Thus the original Unix started to mutate.

In the seventies and to some extent the eighties, Unix was seen by the commercial world as some sort of hippie experiment and was thus shunned. However perhaps like most hippies, it eventually slipped into the mainstream and started to lose its reputation for being badly written and unsecure.

The hardware vendors take interest

Many hardware vendors, including IBM, Hewlett Packard and Data General saw Unix as a way of appeasing their customers. Up until then these customers resented being locked into highly proprietary technology, with no escape route. The marketing pitch from the hardware vendors was that they were giving their clients options. By offering Unix based technology, they were giving their customers an alternative should they feel locked in by the proprietary offerings.

Sounds great, but as we mentioned what customers received was 'Unix plus' so to speak. They got Unix all right, but they got some extra fancy features that were themselves proprietary. Thus the vendor achieved lock-in again, but at the same time making the customer feel in control.

Again over the years there have been quite a few flavours of Unix. Dynix, Ultrix, Irix, Xenix, HP-UX, AIX, Asterix to name a few. Actually the last one is not an operating system, but in fact a cartoon character. Nonetheless a crude rule of thumb is that if the IT buzzword ends in X, it is very likely to have something to do with Unix.

Some exceptions include Solaris, Tru64 and SCO.

Why Unix?

Today Unix is chosen for its reliability. Certain business applications need to be permanently available to the users and customers. Anything less would be damaging to the business. In the modern world such applications typically run on a Unix platform.

But this comes at a cost. Unix is not known for its administrative friendliness. Unlike Windows, which greets you with colour and intuitive icons, Unix greets you with a blank screen and flashing cursor. Whilst one can get a GUI interface for Unix, it is generally used in its 'naked form'. Thus those that administer Unix boxes tend to be at the very smart end of the system administrator spectrum.

3.4 The original Unix administrator?

Interestingly Unix administrators seem to know that and relish it. They appear to speak their own exclusive language. Drop vi, emacs or Korn into a conversation and you get honorary membership. Businesses can thus find them a little unnerving. This is mainly because they appear to do their own thing, get paid a lot and can be a handful to manage. Possibly whilst Unix has evolved technically, culturally it is still rolling in the mud at Woodstock.

So Unix is a very reliable option, but it comes at a cost.

Another relevant point is that Unix is primarily a back-end operating system. Unix on the desktop does exist, but that space is currently dominated by Microsoft Windows.

Linux / Open source

An interesting, and possibly revolutionary, arrival on the scene is a Unix variant called Linux, created by a bright Scandinavian called Linus Torvalds. He put together a variant of Unix based on freely available Unix components.

Source code

At this point I need to introduce another concept called *source code*. When developers write their software, they type instructions into a file via a text editor. This file is known as the source code. To run the software one needs to convert it into binary, as computers only understand ones and zeros. The process of converting the source code into binary (we'll cover how in chapter 5) results in the creation of a binary file. This binary file is more often referred to as an executable file (usually with a suffix .exe). Software vendors traditionally give customers the executable file but not the source file, thus allowing them to run the software. The reason they don't provide the source code is because this would reveal how the software was written. It would be tantamount to giving away their intellectual property. This model of software distribution underpins the software industry.

Well Linus has taken a different approach. He is quite happy to let anybody take a copy of his source code. What's more they can modify it as they see fit. The only demand he makes is that they let him know of the improvements made. This concept is known as copyleft, a funny (well I thought so) variant on copyright. As a result of this magnanimous gesture, hundreds of developers all over the world, in their own free time, are working hard to improve Linux. Consequently Linux is now today one of the most robust variants of Unix. In fact it is currently stealing market share from both Microsoft and its Unix cousins.

The Open Source Movement

Please note that Linus does not appear to be in it for the money. The HR departments of many commercial organizations struggle to pin down where these Unix guys are coming from.

The overall concept of sharing source code in this manner is often referred to as the Open Source movement. It is gaining a lot of advocates in the computing community. Again this has something of a hippie / anarchist feel to it.

It is highly threatening to the likes of Microsoft, who have based their business around the traditional model. What is perhaps more of a concern is that customers may start to demand it (in fact many governments are) and software developers may get caught up in the cult and move to a company that embraces this free spirit attitude.

Microsoft dismissed Linux as a joke at the start of the century. Today they are telling their shareholders that Linux is a threat to their business. The Open

Source movement is gaining traction. Smart companies like SAP, IBM and Oracle are encouraging this movement, though not least to niggle Microsoft.

Open source is more than just Linux, though Linux is the most high profile example. Other examples include Apache (web applications) and Bind (email). Generally open source software is free (freeware) or very very cheap.

This viral approach to evolving open source software produces very robust products. As a result, Linux is the preferred operating system for web-based applications.

Current tensions

This corner of IT is moving at the speed of light. Whilst I mentioned that the Open Group owned the Unix specification, a company called the SCO Group owns the rights to the Unix technology. If I was to choose to write my own version of Unix, Auridianix let's say, I could either write it from scratch using the Open Group specification as my guideline. Or I could licence the technology from SCO Group and possibly add on a few extra 'bells and whistles'.

Remember the specification describes how Unix should work; the technology is the actual software, which is based on the specification.

At the time of writing SCO Group has accused the Linux community of infringing its intellectual property. This is throwing the Unix/Linux market into disarray. One rather large software company is watching this with glee. If it gets its way, Linux and open source will fall from grace and be remembered as nothing more than a romantic notion.

3.5 A pubescent industry

Growing pains

It is worth saying at this point that IT is not like accountancy or farming. As an industry it is going through puberty and we will continue to see these hormonal rushes for some time. IT will have matured when it is used at Board level in sentences that do not also contain the word 'risk' or 'geek'. Again the industry will have settled down once IT becomes more of a utility than an experiment.

The open versus closed source battle is just one of many going on at this moment in time.

Microsoft

Microsoft is a very significant player in the operating system space. It is certainly the most influential vendor and has total control over its operating systems family, thus making the Windows family highly proprietary.

You will recognise some or all of the Windows family tree. We'll take a look at these now.

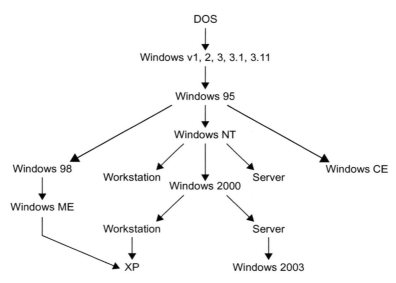

3.6 The Microsoft OS family tree

DOS

In the beginning there was DOS, but it was not good. However it was good enough for IBM to use as the operating system for its personal computer. DOS was Unix-like in that it was not designed with a GUI interface. Thus only IT people and PC enthusiasts bought/used computers during the DOS era.

It stands for Disk Operating System, a name change from QDOS – Quick and Dirty Operating System, which Microsoft, masters of marketing, recognised as far from being a crowd-pleasing title.

Interestingly Microsoft did not invent DOS, they licensed it from Seattle Computer Products. Bill Gates, whilst technically gifted is actually a very shrewd businessman. That may not seem like a particularly revealing comment given that he is a multi-billionaire, but many people do write him off as simply a lucky nerd.

Windows

Windows 1.0 - NT

DOS more or less did the job but looked archaic against the jazzy interface of the Apple Mac. Eventually Microsoft took the GUI interface route and created MS Windows. It went though a number of versions most notably 1.0, 3.1, Windows for Workgroups and eventually Windows 95. Windows 95 was the first 'industrial strength' operating system from Microsoft. It spread quickly throughout the corporate world and essentially drove other would-be desktop contenders out of the game.

It is perhaps timely for us now to have a 2-minute silence for IBM's OS/2, but back to the story.

At this point Microsoft dominated the desktop and so its thoughts turned to the back-end. Thus Windows NT was created, available on the desktop and the server. NT stands for New Technology, but some uncharitable, but perspicacious industry observers suggested it initially stood for 'Not Tested'.

In fairness, after a couple of versions it did prove itself to be a major step forward on the desktop, and whilst not known for its robustness, the back-end offering was impressive in its administrator friendliness. Microsoft's foray into the server market started well and continues to do well.

Windows 2000 - 2003

There was much fanfare regarding the release of Windows 2000, again available on the front and back-end. Strictly speaking it was really just an upgrade to NT but it promised more in respect of security and had a number of features that most corporates did not really have a use for. Thus for many large corporates they are only now getting around to migrating to Windows 2000. Herein lies a lesson; only fashion victims and people who like to debug software products on behalf of the vendor (after they have paid for them) opt for version 1 of anything from Microsoft.

Windows 2003, which is focused on the back-end, has just hit the streets. Most corporations at this stage shouldn't let it into the car park. Having said that the current thaw post the recent technology ice age, during which all upgrades were frozen, is resulting in many organizations hopping from Windows NT to 2003, missing out Windows 2000 in the process.

Windows 98 - XP

Microsoft was also very slow to recognise the potential of the Internet. Its first foray was to try to build a better one (MSN), but the Internet was and is bigger than any single vendor. MSN embraces the very popular HoTMaiL email service.

Its second attempt was to create an Internet embracing operating system called Windows 98. It was a knee-jerk reaction; version 1 did not actually work. So Microsoft made it a consumer product, as 'Joe Public' was unlikely to complain as much as corporates.

98 evolved to ME (Millennium Edition), which was fine. But Microsoft now had a problem in that it had mutated its desktop operating system into two parallel product lines. To get the desktop back on the one track it created Windows XP (eXPerience). Whilst it is being sold to corporates, its rich multimedia capability looks more geared to the consumer, unless you actually need your staff to watch DVDs all day.

So today we have Windows 2003 for the back-end and Windows XP for the desktop.

Windows CE

But Microsoft, concerned about its traditional power base, the PC (more on this later) is actively looking to find a new platform. It has created Windows CE (Compact Edition), which is designed to run on non-standard computing devices such as mobile phones, fridges and TVs. It has yet to gain any real traction in the marketplace, but this may reflect its relative lack of influence in these areas rather than the market regarding it as being technically inferior. In any case Microsoft is pushing CE very hard.

So you can see, Microsoft is quite a player in the operating system world.

Other Proprietary Operating systems

To some extent this category is for those operating systems that:

❑ Were great in their time

❑ Existed prior to Windows and Unix

❑ Sit on the sidelines of the main operating system marketplace.

IBM

IBM is a major force in computing with similar revenues to Microsoft, though far less profitable. In many respects IBM taught Microsoft how to sell IT products. IBM was the company to hate/envy/distrust before Microsoft. Its aggressive approach to business development made it something of a role model for Microsoft.

IBM's hardware product range is so extensive that it could have quite easily created its own ecosystem. Sadly it was so proprietary that even its own bits of kit wouldn't link together. This lack of cohesion led to a plethora of operating systems. Over the years these have included: MVS, CMS, ESA, OS/36, OS/38, OS/360, OS/390, OS/400, OS/2.

As yet IBM has not realised the marketing value of giving operating systems business-friendly names. Even IBM's Warp operating system was named to appeal to Trekkies. Some say it was destroyed by the vortex created by its own irrelevance. The truth was that it was ahead of its time, but technology is a poor second cousin to marketing.

DEC

Another titan of the 'big hair, side burns and flairs' era was Digital Equipment Corporation (Dec). Dec was number two only to IBM and was smart enough to at least have compatibility within its own product range.

One of its earliest computers was the PDP-11. The one I used didn't even have a standard desktop interface. The user terminal was like a sewing machine workstation with a teletype terminal as opposed to monitor. Thus the 'screen' was printed onto paper! This mini computer was one of the first computers to run Unix.

But DEC is probably best remembered by its Vax family of midrange to mainframe computers. The DEC Vax ran an operating system called VMS. This was remarkably robust, relatively intuitive, but amazingly, 20 years ago could enable Vaxes to be clustered together to act like one big super computer (See Grid Computing in chapter 7). They don't make them anymore, but like Renault 5's you will still occasionally see them on the road. Although not literally in the case of Vaxes, so spotting them would not make a great car game for bored kids on long journeys.

Figure 3.7 Reminiscing over a Vax VMS operator's manual

DEC also developed a reputation for building fault-tolerant computers, ie ones that would run 24 x 7. But the two players who had this as their core business were Stratus with the VOS operating system and Tandem with the appropriately named NonStop. NB. Tandem was acquired by Compaq.

Latterly Dec created the Alpha server. By this point Dec had a range of operating systems: VMS, Mumps, OpenVMS, Ultrix and OSF/1. However despite being an early adopter of Unix, it failed to see its market importance. It also chose to ignore the emergence of the PC, dismissing it as a consumer device. Its subsequent implosion caused it to fall into the hands of Compaq, which by the way in recent times fell into the hands of Hewlett Packard (Now HP).

HP prior to its Unix variant HP-UX had MPE.

The rest

Other names include VME and George from ICL, now owned by Fujitsu.

An extinct company called Prime had an operating system called Primos.

Apple has something called MacOS.

McDonald Douglas had something called Pick.

Even Marconi's parent GEC had an operating system called GCOS.

This is still a far from complete list. Many of the operating systems mentioned in this section are now receiving their pension. The smart money is on Windows or Unix. Though IBM may have a view on this.

In summary

- ❑ Software needs hardware to run
- ❑ Software can be classified into operating system and application software
- ❑ Operating system standardisation is a key issue for businesses
- ❑ Unix and Windows are the key operating system families in the commercial world

- ❏ Linux is threatening to redefine the operating system marketplace
- ❏ Open source is threatening to redefine the software industry
    - ○ Nobody can predict the future.

Test yourself?

9. An operating system is:
    a. A legacy of a bygone era, and never used in modern IT systems
    b. Really hardware
    c. Makes the computer usable
    d. Is restricted to surgical procedures

10. Application software:
    a. Is perceived as useful by the users
    b. Is sold with its own operating system
    c. Just focuses on ERP, CRM and SCM
    d. Is always sold on a 'plug and go' basis.

11. The fundamental framework:
    a. Is a hardware-only concept
    b. Was developed in Amsterdam
    c. Details how applications, operating systems and hardware fit together
    d. Microsoft is the number one fundamental framework supplier.

12. Unix:
    a. Is really a family of operating systems
    b. Was developed by Xerox
    c. Is controlled by Microsoft
    d. Spawned the open source operating system Linux.

13. Microsoft:
   a. Created the first ever 'Intel based' PC
   b. Gave IBM its first big break in the marketplace
   c. Is a major player in the operating systems marketplace
   d. Refuses to extend its operating system to servers.

Chapter 4

Application Software

Why read this? This chapter explains what application software is, the forms that it takes and why it is valuable to organizations.

Key to business

You need to get a report to your boss? Do you care what platform the word processor runs on? A trader at an investment bank, does she care what operating system their trade management software runs on? In both cases it is a resounding 'no'. Users only care about what helps them to:

- ❏ Do their job
- ❏ Make money
- ❏ Cut costs
- ❏ Save time
- ❏ Look good.

The stuff that achieves this is known as application software. Of course the application software needs a platform made up of hardware and an operating system, but as far as businesses are concerned the value of IT to them is in the application software. In short application software is where the money is most likely to be found in the IT industry.

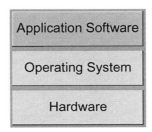

4.1 Application software

Software engineers, programmers, developers, call them what you will also write operating systems (OS) as well as application software. But there are far fewer OS specialists because the number of operating systems in the world is miniscule compared to the number of applications. So the bulk of software related activity in business is in the development and maintenance of application software.

Businesses can either:

- ❑ Write their own software
- ❑ Buy packaged software
- ❑ Buy software tailored to their particular needs
- ❑ Buy existing software that needs tuning to meet their specific needs.

In terms of software production, we will see how this is achieved in chapter 5. Let us look now at the manner in which software vendors serve up their wares.

Packaged software

Packaged software is sometimes referred to as:

- ❑ 'Off the Shelf' (OTS)
- ❑ 'Shrink wrapped'
- ❑ 'Over the counter'

4.2 Packaged software

As the phrases imply this is software that one can buy in a store. Another perspective is that packaged software is 'write once sell many times' software. The vendor spots a market and develops a generic product that meets the needs of as much of that market as possible. The most successful example of this is MS Office.

Plug and chug

The idea is that once bought you do not need a team of system integrators to load it up onto your machine (your experiences may seem somewhat different).

The software should just 'plug and chug'.

Everyone's a winner

Both the vendor and the buyer should be winners here. Once the vendor has covered their development costs, each package sold over and above this is almost 100% pure profit. It's the business to be in but you need to be very sure of your market.

The buyer gets the benefit of a sophisticated product without having to incur the full development costs. In fact she has probably shared the development costs with thousands if not millions of others.

The game for the vendor is getting the right balance re pricing. Microsoft has been 'stretching the envelope' of late to ensure that it is not being unnecessarily generous. The market has been quick to share its feelings.

Because packaged software needs to meet the need of a sufficiently wide market to be profitable it is often over-engineered with functionality to widen its market attractiveness. Thus many users have a sense of being novice users because they feel they have only mastered a fraction of the functionality they have paid for.

Another key point here is that in respect to MS Office the market generally had what it needed with Office 95. However we have been bounced along to Office XP at great cost in respect of new software and underlying hardware. Users are waking up to this. Microsoft in particular will see a slow down in product version turnover. It will be interesting to see how Microsoft responds to this.

Tailored software

Scenario - NASA needs to put a ferret on Mars. They can't go out to PC World and ask for ferret life support and telemetry software (Martian edition). That's not a reflection on PC World but on the fact that no software vendor in their right mind would develop such software, because there is at best a market of, in this case, one.

4.3 Tailored software

So NASA needs to either build the software itself or subcontract the job to an external supplier. This is an example of tailored software. 'Write once sell once', or more specifically 'sell once then write once'.

Such software is sometimes referred to as bespoke software. Imagine you are buying clothes. Either your dimensions warrant personal tailoring or you are simply happy to share your wealth with a tailor.

Businesses only revert to tailored software as a last resort. By having tailored software written they are exposing themselves to the following:

- ❑ The full development costs
- ❑ Delay as they wait for the software to be built
- ❑ Software that has never been tested in 'battlefield' conditions

But companies do this because they do not have any other options.

Customised software

The downsides of having a fully tailored solution from the buyers perspective, coupled with the frustration of building a system and only selling it once from the vendor's perspective, has led to what might be called the hybrid or customised software market.

4.4 Customised software

This can evolve in one of two ways.

Resold bespoke solution

The vendor builds for example an expensive trading system for an investment bank. The vendor agrees with the bank that it is allowed to resell the software to other banks and for each sale it pays a royalty to the investment bank. Thus the original customer has the option of reducing its initial investment, and who knows, creating a new revenue stream.

But why would it do that? Surely by doing so it will be losing its competitive advantage? In practice most customers take the view that it is their people and not the software that delivers the competitive advantage. They are also attracted by the fact that they are taking their competitors' money.

80:20

The alternative approach is more proactive. The software company surveys the market as if they were a packaged software vendor. But instead of looking to meet one hundred percent of the needs of the market, it aims for 80 percent. You might have heard of the 80:20 rule, or Pareto Principle. In relation to software, 80% of the value is in 20% of the software. So such enterprising vendors have gone to market with products that give their customers 80% of what they need. They also point out to the customer that the price will be 20% of the cost of writing the software themselves. This looks like a good deal.

But the real clincher is that most big companies will say we like the 80% you are giving us, but we also want the 20% that is peculiar to our business. This is where the hybrid vendors start salivating, because if we apply the Pareto principle again, this 20% of extra functionality is going to become circa 80% of the final cost.

This is such a clever model that I am surprised that Microsoft hasn't adopted it? Well in fact it has. By acquiring Great Plains and Navision it has entered this marketplace. And if Microsoft thinks this is the way to go then there might just be something in it. Microsoft's dalliance with Sap reinforces this.

Enterprise Applications

A particular variant of this hybrid marketplace is known as Enterprise Applications (EA). The founding company was a German software player called SAP. Their roots were in manufacturing and they recognised that 80% of what manufacturers did was the same in most manufacturing companies. They thus created software modules to address these common functions. They looked beyond manufacturing into HR, Sales, Marketing, Finance and lo the same applied. Thus they were able to go to market with a complete end-to-end enterprise solution.

Other players in this space include PeopleSoft (guess which department they started out in?), Oracle, Siebel, Baan to name but a few. The enterprise applications marketplace has matured to such an extent that there are now three very overlapping categories of EAs.

Lets take a look at them:

ERP (Enterprise Resource Planning)

Ignore the expanded acronym, as it shines no light on the subject whatsoever. This was the first wave of enterprise applications and focused on helping businesses:

- ❑ Link up their departments
- ❑ Get better value through a more centralised approach to managing the data

4.5 ERP - Joining up the business

Before IT strategy

The problem that ERP was solving stemmed from the fact that prior to the nineties IT was not considered as a strategic part of the business. Consequently different departments did their own thing regarding IT. HR, for example may have run their personnel management software on a Windows box, whereas Finance may have had their payroll software developed in-house to run on a Unix server.

Scenario: A new person joins the business. HR enters their data but now has to phone up Finance in order to put the new entrant onto the payroll. Their systems were technologically incompatible and were never designed to interoperate (English: work together).

ERP vendors arrived with this software solution that enabled an organization to resolve these issues by simply sprinkling software modules across all the departments.

Y2K and management control

The centralisation of the corporate data meant that for the first time the business leaders could truly see what was going on in the business. In later years this concept has grown into what is known as the 'digital dashboard'.

Thus it was an easy 'sell' to business leaders. Couple this to the fact that Y2K was imminent, ERP proved a more attractive step forward than fixing your existing legacy systems. So in the run up to Y2K (1st January 2000 – Remember the day that planes did not fall out of the sky?) the market couldn't get enough of ERP.

Subsequently it has gone through a series of declines and revivals. But for many of the ERP players the opportunities lie in CRM and SCM, which we will look at next.

CRM (Customer Relationship Management)

This acronym at least has some meaning. CRM is more than just a technology solution, and this is what made it such a compelling 'sell'.

A philosophy

CRM is more a business philosophy, which has the following tenets:

- It is easier to get business from existing customers than new ones
- 20% of your customers give you 80% of the business
- Everyone in the business needs to be customer-facing
- Customers need/want to be managed.

4.6 CRM - Keep your best customers happy

As a philosophy, it is just a viewpoint, and not an absolute truth. In fact there are many situations were none of these tenets would hold true, particularly the last bullet.

However there are also many cases where these hold strong. Enterprise application vendors have latched onto this and have created a suite of software modules that:

- Gives everyone access to customer data
  - o From call centre through to Board
- Ensure customer data is only stored once in the corporate database
- Provide tools to predict what customers will do next, based on what they have done in the past.

Both sales and marketing software have been available for some time. US player Siebel saw the opportunity and took this to the enterprise level and thus created the CRM marketplace.

A compelling offering

CRM was a compelling offering as far as business leaders/owners were concerned. Now with the press of a button they could identify who their best customers were, and devote their limited resources to them. In other words rather than:

- ❏ Treating all customers equally
- ❏ Spending most of their resources managing high hassle, low margin clients, businesses could focus on high margin, low hassle customers.

A waste of money

This all feels great. However it hasn't worked. At the time of writing, according to Gartner Group, 40% of CRM systems lie unused. The following reasons are most likely to be the cause:

- ❏ The buyer presumed that a new CRM system would turn bad sales people into good ones
  - o When in fact it just made them more efficiently bad
- ❏ The buyer did not train the users
- ❏ The buyer did not integrate the CRM software into the appropriate sales and marketing business processes
- ❏ The sales people in particular did not want to play the game of sharing customer intelligence
  - o What is the benefit to them as individuals in sharing their 'crown jewels' with the rest of the organization? It's a sales thing.

Thus CRM today leaves the same bad taste in one's mouth as broadband mobile phone technology. It over promised and under delivered.

It's IT's fault

Worst of all, the IT department gets the blame for this, even though the technology does the job. The IT department has provided the business tool, as requested. The business has (in circa 40% of the cases) failed to use the tool effectively.

CRM is still a good idea for many businesses. However the business needs to be aware of how much investment is required, over and above the purchase of the software, to make it work.

SCM (Supply Chain Management)

Again the acronym does describe the concept. This is all about driving costs out of the business, which is a key theme in this post dotcom world.

From mine to showroom

Think showroom to raw materials. For example:

- ❑ The customer orders a car
- ❑ The showroom liases with the manufacturer
- ❑ The manufacturer liases with the component suppliers
  - ○ Eg. Tyres, lights, engines
- ❑ The component supplier liases with the raw materials suppliers
  - ○ Eg. For rubber, steel, leather.

4.7 SCM - Timely delivery

Application Software

Every company has a supply chain, or sits on someone else's supply chain. Thus it is a theme relevant to all businesses.

Retail leads the way

Certain sectors like Retail have always been hot on this. They play a good defensive game, ie they try not to spend more money than they have to. Today retailers are so efficient that they are generally looking to shave off fractions of a penny in each transaction they make.

But if one looks at sectors such as Finance, Pharmaceuticals, Oil and Gas, they have never been too focused on cost management because they have always played offensive. That is to say they have been more focused on sales than cost management. Their approach to cash flow management was/is to stoke the front-office of the business rather than the back-office.

Difficult times

In a difficult economic climate, it is not so easy to play offensive, and hence the timing for SCM solutions post dotcom is good. This is likely to evolve in a number of steps:

- ❑ Straight Through Processing – Automate the existing back office functions
    - o A lot of activity here
- ❑ Utilise internal exchanges for procuring items such as stationery
    - o Some activity here
- ❑ Utilise external exchanges for real-time dynamic procurement
    - o Romantic notion oversold during dotcom era.

In my humble opinion, SCM is where the growth is. All the vendors want to lead this area. Because everyone cannot be number one, we are seeing this area fragment into micro niches, such as:

- ❑ Supply Chain Planning
- ❑ Supply Chain Execution
- ❑ Enterprise Profit Optimisation.

Key players include i2, CommerceOne, Ariba and Manugistics. Ultimately all the SCM vendors will be the number one supplier in a myriad of niches.

RFID

Radio Frequency Identification is the latest hot term. In essence it is next generation bar coding, using wireless technology. It will play a key role in SCM, but there is a danger that the market will expect too much of it. Similarly unless a universal standard is agreed, it will be constrained to niche/supplier specific situations.

Remember application software is the reason why businesses use IT. Everything else plays a supporting role to this.

In summary

- ❑ Acquiring software can be achieved in four ways:
  - o Produce in-house
  - o Buy packaged software
  - o Buy tailored software
  - o Buy hybrid software.
- ❑ Enterprise applications is the most high profile example of hybrid software
- ❑ The most high profile categories of enterprise applications software are:
  - o ERP
    - ▪ The market was disillusioned, but has come back for more
  - o CRM
    - ▪ The market is currently disillusioned
  - o SCM
    - ▪ The market has yet to be disillusioned.

83

Test yourself?

14. Application software:
     a. Is of no interest to the user
     b. Is synonymous with packaged software
     c. Makes the computer useful
     d. Is only sold by Microsoft

15. Other names for packaged software include:
     a. Brown paper bag
     b. Off the shelf
     c. Over the counter
     d. Under the counter.

16. Tailored software:
     a. Is only ever required by Nasa
     b. Tends to be path taken by cost conscious customers
     c. Is chosen solely by large corporations to impress clients
     d. Can be expensive.

17. CRM:
     a. Buyers of CRM software recognise that it is easier to get business from existing clients
     b. All clients love to be managed
     c. Is a quick win approach to turning your bad sales force into a good one
     d. Needs to be integrated into one's organization with care.

18. SCM:
     a. Will be of interest to procurement officers
     b. Has no place in the world of financial services
     c. Is very in tune with today's economic realities
     d. Has resulted in online public exchanges revolutionising the way business is conducted.

Section 2

Application Development
The importance of programming languages and databases

Why applications are so important to business and how they are built.

☐ Chapter 5 – Application Development

Chapter 5

Application Development

Why read this? The real value in IT comes from application software. Understanding the associated technologies, namely programming languages and databases, will provide a useful insight into the production process.

Overview

To recap, application software is a key element of an organization's IT investment. It can be thought of as the stuff that makes the IT investment useful to the users/business.

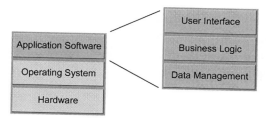

5.1 Elements of the application layer

Earlier on we looked at the fundamental framework and saw that the application software sat on top of the operating system and hardware. See diagram 5.1. As you can see from the diagram, the application layer itself can be partitioned into 3 layers as follows:

User interface

This part of the application deals with the user interaction. The quality of the user interface determines the user experience and so is critical to the effectiveness of the application.

Prior to the arrival of the PC, the user interface typically comprised a dark green screen with light green text. This character-based interface restricted IT usage to technologists.

The arrival of the WIMP (Windows Icons Menu Pop-ups) or GUI (Graphical User Interface) made applications more user friendly.

Think of the user interface as that part of the application that enables the user to enter data and retrieve information.

The user interface is developed using a programming language. More details are provided later on in the chapter.

Developing the user interface is both art and science. Not all techies are adept at producing intuitive interfaces that are neither patronizing nor terrifying.

Business logic

The business logic can be thought of as the clever part of the application. This is where the data input into the application is processed. Whereas the user interface is focused on usability the business logic is focused on algorithmic neatness. The algorithm is the software that carries out the processing.

A good example of this would be an application designed to calculate health insurance policy premiums. The user interface captures the relevant information, for example name, age, previous illnesses, units of alcohol consumed and so on. Once captured this data is 'fed' to the health insurance policy premium algorithm, which calculates the premium and presents the figure to the user via the user interface.

Thus the business logic is the clever part of the application and the people that are good at this aspect of programming tend to have an intimate understanding of the business context in which the application will be used.

Please note that in many cases it is the same programmer that develops the user interface and the business logic. But in some cases, particularly, where the application is very sophisticated, different people with different skills will cover each layer of the application.

Like the user interface, the business logic is developed using a programming language. In some but not all cases the same programming language is used for both layers.

The majority of IT systems in use can be described as administrative. That is to say there is very little business logic. The users simply enter data into the system and it is stored with very little processing taking place. Examples include:

- Personnel management systems
- Customer relationship management systems
- Procurement systems

However some systems have very complex business logic. These include:

- Car management systems
- Fighter aircraft weapons systems
- Space station life support systems.

Typically but not always these systems tend to be categorized as 'real-time'. Such systems tend to take data from their environment and respond (very quickly) to significant changes.

Data management

The final layer of the application is the data management layer. An application that doesn't have a data management component is very likely to be trivial/calculator based. Thus all computer-based applications have to manage data.

In essence data management means:

- Data storage
- Data access.

Take our insurance policy example. Once the data entered by the user is processed it will be stored along with the calculated premium. This will enable the policy company to produce the relevant documents and to keep track of the transaction. Even if the user does not accept the policy, storing the policy data will:

- Save the user from having to re enter all their details should they decide to pursue a policy quote at a later date
- Enable the policy company to study the profiles of users who do not immediately accept the calculated quote.

The data management element of the application is developed using database technology.

To recap:

- User interface – Data input/output
  - Delivered using programming language technology
- Business logic – Data processing
  - Delivered using programming language technology
- Data management – Data management.
  - Delivered using database technology

Consequently programming languages and databases exist to enable the production of application software. We will now take a look at these in turn:

Programming Languages

Overview

We all use language for communication. There are many languages offering different ways to:

- Conduct basic communication: hello, goodbye, thank you….
- Present arguments in a reasonable manner: If, but, then….

Some languages are better than others for certain purposes:

- French / Italian for romantic situations
- English (UK) for understatement
- English (US) for controlling manned space programmes.

5.2 Titled – Boss programming member of staff

These languages have evolved/mutated in a somewhat Darwinian manner. They have adapted to the environments in which they are used. And so it is with programming languages.

Programming languages exist to enable the programmers to communicate with the computer. They enable the programmer to instruct the computer to carry out specific actions, eg. Add two numbers or calculate the landing point of an incoming comet.

Again they generally offer different ways to:

- Conduct basic communication: Open file, Print, Close file
- Present logic
  - Loop – FOR x=1 TO 10, PRINT x
  - Make decisions – IF x>5 THEN PRINT "Hello"
  - Selection – CASE x=1 PRINT "YES"; CASE x=2 PRINT "NO"; CASE x=3 PRINT "Maybe"

Please note there are many different language types in IT. These include:

- Querying languages
  - Eg. SQL

- ❏ Communication languages
  - o Eg. TCP/IP
- ❏ Formatting languages
  - o Eg. HTML.

None of these are programming languages. Why? Because they do not include the decision-making capability described above, ie. the ability to loop, select and make decisions. The power of programming languages is their ability to produce sophisticated and flexible algorithms that can be applied to any business and even scientific situation.

Examples of algorithms include:

- ❏ Sorting a set of dates into chronological order
- ❏ Simulating atomic particle collisions.

There are many programming languages in use today. Again they have been created to address the needs of the environment in which they will be used. In broad terms programming languages are often optimised to:

- ❏ Perform numeric calculations
- ❏ Produce beautiful user interfaces
- ❏ Perform at great speed. Key for real-time applications
- ❏ Manipulate data.

Most languages address some of these, but the degree to which they do them all well varies.

Programming languages have evolved over time. We will look at this a little later as it shines light on the portfolio of programming languages used by organizations today.

Compilers

Modern computers are based on digital technology. Digital is synonymous with binary. Binary is a numbering system where there are only two values, one and zero. These can be represented as Yes and No or True and False. Compare this with the more common numbering system denary, ten symbols 0

– 9, invented by the Romans and the principal system used today for numerical activities.

All data is stored on computers as binary as are computer programs. For a program to run it needs to be in binary format. The file in which the binary code is stored is known as the binary, object or executable file.

But as we have seen programmers use words like IF, THEN, UNTIL, which enable modern computer programs to read like structured English. The programmer writes their program into what is known as a source file.

Thus programmers need to somehow convert source files into binary files if they want their programs to run on a computer.

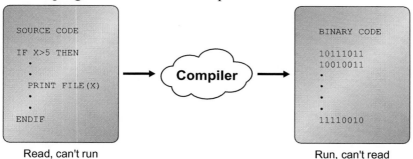

Read, can't run   Run, can't read

5.3 The role of the compiler

The tool to achieve this translation is called a compiler. A compiler is a piece of software that translates source code into binary code. Compilers are aligned to programming languages, so we have for example Cobol, C, C++ compilers.

Where a programming language has become a vendor independent standard, for example C, Cobol and C++, the compiler can be purchased from more than one vendor. Thus there is a market for developing C compilers. A few languages are platform independent. For example C, which is available on PCs, Unix servers and mainframes. So not only is there a market for C compilers, but there are specific markets for C compilers on each platform.

Compilers are a key element of software development and consequently this is a big business. There are also plenty of proprietary languages, ie those that are under the control of a single vendor. Visual Basic is a good example. It only runs on Windows based platforms and is only available from Microsoft. Thus there is no compiler market for VB.

The process of compilation takes place during the development phase. The act of compilation could be done as the program runs, line by line, but this slows it down. Where this happens, the compiler is known as an Interpreter. These are rarely used in commercial computing.

We are focused here on application software, but remember that operating systems are also software and so they also need to be programmed and compiled.

Remember compilers are software programs themselves. If you are of a philosophical disposition why not spend a few hours considering how programmers write compilers? Alternatively attend our IT Demystified seminar.

The Evolution of programming languages

As the IT industry has evolved so have programming languages. Their evolution reflects both advances in technology and the need for greater productivity in respect of software development.

Machine code

We have already mentioned that computers only understand binary, ie. ones and zeros. When computers were first invented they were literally programmed in binary, otherwise known as machine code.

The input mechanism to the computer was not a keyboard but a line of switches; typically 8 or 16 in a row. By the way, the monitor wasn't a TV-like visual display unit (VDU for those that like their IT text books written using outdated thirty year old acronyms), but a printer. Anyway to programme the computer the programmer needed to flick each switch up for one and down for zero. Once the line of switches were set the enter button was pressed and the program instruction was entered into the program memory.

Not only was this tedious it was neurosurgery. Make one mistake and it was start again time. Up switch, up switch, up switch, down switch, up switch, down switch, whoops (or such like). NB A typical program would comprise many instructions and starting again was quite unattractive.

Debugging a program back then was something of a challenge. Can you guess what the problem is with the following program extract?

1011011101101100

1111000011110000

0000101010101010

1111000011110000

1111111111110000

5.4 An example of binary code

You now know what it felt like to be a machine code programmer.

To make life a little easier the computers used to print out the machine code in hexadecimal. We have mentioned binary (base 2 counting system) and denary (base 10 counting system). Hexadecimal is base 16. 0 to 9 is represented as 0 to 9. However 10 to 15 is represented as A to F.

0 - 9	10	11	12	13	14	15
0 - 9	A	B	C	D	E	F

5.5 The role of the compiler

So 1 is represented as 1 in hex and 15 is represented as F. 16 is represented as 10, 17 as 11, 26 as 1A and so on. For more details ask a cryptologist or a baby-boomer programmer.

So a typical machine code dump (ie print out) might look like the following:

13A4

BBCD

1128

E0E6

99AF

5.6 An example of hexadecimal code

95

Admittedly this still doesn't shine much light on what is going on from a programming perspective, but at least hex is less hungry on ink.

Machine code is very computer specific and so the machine code from one computer will not run on a computer with a different computer processor (technically known as the CPU, eg. Pentium II).

The world of computing was restricted to people with brains the size of planets. And even these bright sparks had limited productivity given the tedium of entering the program onto the computer.

Fortunately there is no commercial requirement to machine code program these days.

Machine code is often referred to as a 1GL or a 1st Generation Language. It should be of no surprise that there isn't a Zeroth Generation Language.

Assembler

Assembler was an attempt to improve programming productivity. Rather than programming in ones and zeros, a set of commands were created that shone some light on what the programmer was instructing the computer to do.

These lines of assembler are converted by the computer into machine code, because 'at the end of the day' computers still only understand binary.

Whilst assembler was a quantum leap in programmer friendliness it was still a far cry from being developer friendly. An example of machine code follows:

ADD 1,2

JMP, 2

SHR, 7

STR, 3

5.7 An example of assembler

Again this is not particularly intuitive. But once the commands (aka instruction set) are understood it is, in relative terms, a joy to use.

Another benefit with assembler is that it gives a circa 1000% increase in productivity. A line of assembler translates into circa 10 lines of machine code.

Assembler like machine code is CPU specific. Assembler languages normally adopt this mnemonic format, ie the commands are short forms of the instruction, eg. JMP means Jump and SHR means Shift Right. But there are also algebraic notations eg. V1 + V6 = V8. The instructions look more like formulae. Please note that you do not need to know any of this paragraph, I am just being nostalgic.

Assembler is still in use today. Assembler programs are difficult, and therefore costly, to maintain, but they run like the wind and so are used where speed is of the essence. Thus assembler is often associated with real-time systems. It is however also associated with old systems, particularly in the worlds of Finance and Space.

Assembler programming languages are known as 2GLs or 2nd Generation languages.

High level

As computing gathered traction as a productivity tool, the need for software applications grew. In order to improve software development productivity and make programming more accessible to people with conventional sized brains, programming instructions were created that looked a lot more like English. The term high-level was coined for these languages.

High-level languages were considered sufficiently 'dumbed down' to enable Joe (and Josephine) Public to try their hand. If you are over thirty you may well have fond memories of programming in Basic on your Sinclair ZX81 or Commodore64. Words like Atari, Amiga and Tandy might well cause you to get a 'full on' nostalgia attack. Alternatively you might have been one of these people who preferred to mix with other people in your youth. The price you have paid for your enhanced social skills is the inability to programme in Basic, Logo, Lisp and Pascal. Your loss.

Think of high-level languages as being somewhat 'Starsky and Hutch' in design. They came to light in the seventies in a pre-PC era. Consequently programmers were using these 3GLs to write software that would have its user interface displayed on a dumb terminal. As a result programming languages were weak on user interface development, as the operating systems of the day could not handle WIMP or GUI interfaces.

Other examples of 3GLs include:

- C
- C++
- Fortran
- Algol
- Smalltalk
- Cobol
- Ada
- Perl
- Jovial

5.8 Examples of 3GLs

C and C++ are still popular today. Cobol has peaked, but there is still a lot of it about. Perl has found a niche in the world of web applications. The rest are museum items.

An example of 3GL programming, which you may well have written yourself on your first computer follows:

```
X=0
Y=0
FOR X= 1 TO 10 STEP 1
        Y= X+Y
        PRINT Y
ENDFOR
```

5.9 An example of 3GL source code

Again this is no 'page turner' in terms of readability, but it is much more intuitive than assembler and machine code. Just out of interest this program loops 10 times with X increasing in value by 1 each time. For each loop Y is printed once it has added the latest value of X to the previous value of Y. Again this is more detail than you really need. I am just trying to make you regret your misspent computer-free youth!

Third generation languages are very popular today. Speed being their main attribute. 3GL compilers have had thirty years to get fast and bug free. In new applications they are very much associated with the business logic layer of the software.

Another key point about high-level languages was that for the first time the programmer did not have to understand what was going on in the underlying hardware. Prior to 3GL software experts had to be hardware experts.

The upside of this was that software was more portable between different computers, so long as compilers existed on both platforms for the language used.

The downside was that the programmer being one step removed from the hardware was unable to optimise their software for the underlying platform and if there were problems in the development process they would be unable to ascertain whether the problem related to the software or the hardware. This was a big issue when memory and processing power were very expensive. Today it is not much of an issue given the reliability of hardware and most compilers.

Visual

The arrival of the GUI interface heralded the dawn of the computer as an intuitive productivity tool. Unfortunately 3GL programming languages, whilst powerful from a business logic perspective were weak from a user interface perspective. Ask anyone who has had the misfortune to create a forms-based interface using Fortran. The simple act of putting a name field (ie a field in which the user can enter their name) on a screen was a time consuming job.

- ❑ Step 1 Programme the screen coordinates on which the field is to be located. This in itself is an exercise in extra sensory perception.

- ❏ Step 2 Compile the screen code
- ❏ Step 3 Run the screen code to see if the field is where you expected it to be.
- ❏ Step 4 Repeat Steps 1 to 3 until the field is correctly positioned.

Any user that even suggested that the background colour be anything other than the natural colour of the screen (usually dark green) would be given short shrift.

Thus 3GLs did not allow programmers to exploit the intuitive interface of a GUI oriented operating system.

This prompted the arrival of the 4GL, which can be described as a 3GL with GUI development capability. With such visual languages, positioning fields was a simple exercise in dragging the field onto the form and dropping it where you wanted. If it didn't look quite right tickle it along with the mouse.

The user could have any colour they wanted, including Alpine and lunar backgrounds. Dealing with finicky and indecisive users was now more bearable for the programmer.

Perhaps most importantly 4GLs enabled users to see what they were getting in respect of the systems 'look and feel' at a very early stage of the development process, rather than having to wait until the system was delivered in full. Thus 4GLs made prototyping much easier.

Another advancement with 4GLs was the inclusion of commands that made it easier to manipulate data held in databases. Rather than having to write one's own database, it was possible to use standard commands provided by the programming language to perform database related operations such as opening, searching, updating and closing on commercially available databases.

Both the visual and data manipulation advancements in 4GLs enabled great leaps in programmer productivity. All modern standard computer applications are built with a GUI interface and consequently a 4GL.

Examples of 4GLs include:

- Visual Basic
- PowerBuilder
- Delphi
- Visual C++
- Foxpro
- DBase

5.10 Examples of 4GLs

4GLs have generally embraced the concept of object orientation (See Chapter 5), though admittedly to varying degrees. Nonetheless the romantic notion of building systems using reusable components is better supported by 4GLs than 3GLs. But please note that object orientation is not a 4GL concept. C++ is a 3GL and is one of the most popular object oriented programming languages of the last 30 years. Please also note that it is also possible to write object oriented machine code, but this is not recommended.

If you have ever pondered on the difference between Basic and Visual Basic or C++ and Visual C++, you now know the answer, the word 'visual' is often used as a clue in IT circles for something that pertains to the user interface. Visual C++ is thus a more GUI development friendly version of C++. Similarly with Visual Basic and Basic. Full marks to Microsoft, creator of the two visual examples mentioned. They have successfully turned two vendor independent 3GLs into two very vendor dependent 4GLs.

Java

I am sure you are asking yourself where does Java fit into all of this? Java doesn't really fit the traditional model because it is a 3GL that was developed in the nineties. But given that the GUI based interface was well established by then, why was it not created as a 4GL?

The answer lies in the reasoning behind its creation. Those clever people at Sun Microsystems had known for some time that the days of computing being constrained to computers was drawing to a close. They saw a future where computing existed within cars, fridges, pens and even tablets. Such items did not have a conventional keyboard/monitor interface, as they would not require user or even operator intervention. Once the software was written, it would go about its business behind the scenes.

Java was created for that vision of computing beyond computers and so was not developed with in-built GUI development capability. In that respect it is a 3GL.

Despite Java's raison d'etre, the commercial world saw it primarily as a programming language that was optimised for networking based applications (see chapter 10) and hence it became strongly associated with web based application development.

In recent years Sun has recognised its usefulness in the traditional world of computing and has extended the language to include GUI development. So this extended Java can be thought of as a 4GL.

4GLs are very popular in commercial computing, particularly in respect of user interface development. They of course have the capability to produce the business logic as well and are often used for that purpose.

However if speed of processing is important it is very likely that a 3GL will be used for the business logic. So it would not be surprising to hear of an application being built using more than one programming language.

Artificial intelligence

The final generation (to date) of programming languages are known as 5GLs. The whole evolutionary model of programming languages falls apart at this stage. The main reasons being that:

❑ There is very little development activity in respect of progressing 5GLs. Most 5GLs are really 3GL-like in many respects

❑ The market that they were to fuel has failed to evolve.

In summary 5GLs can be defined as programming languages that are knowledge-based. They provide the capability to capture and leverage information. You might say that this capability is nothing more than that of a

4GL. Well if you had been a little bit more patient, I would have added that ... cue the X Files theme tune... that they can also learn.

Learning is the scary bit. Previous generations of languages simply did what they were told by the programmer. They did not think for themselves and in that sense were stupid.

Imagine a piece of software that concludes that its author was less than smart and then evolves itself to solve what it believes to be the problem at hand. That is unnerving.

Leaving you to ponder on the possibilities, I will return to the mundane fact that 5GLs were created to enable programmers to build smarter software. Such software was to find its way into robots and expert systems that would replace the need for human experts such as lawyers, architects and doctors.

The buzzwords that come to mind in respect of 5GLs are knowledge, artificial intelligence and expert systems.

Robots have evolved very little beyond Tamagotchi toys, though admittedly they are fascinating. Expert systems extend to case-based reasoning, which rather than having one expert lawyer; you have a room full of lawyers that each has experience of one legal scenario.

The only languages that come to mind in respect of 5GLs are Lisp and Prolog and these are relatively ancient.

There have been some very positive advances in artificial intelligence, but these are not underpinned by 5GLs. Examples include:

- ❑ Biometrics – Using distinguishing human characteristics to uniquely identify people
- ❑ Fuzzy logic – Whereas computers think in ones and zeros (true and false), humans think in terms of degrees of truth. Computers using fuzzy logic can draw conclusions by building up enough evidence based on partial truths. Imagine you are on the beach and you have wrapped yourself around a few cocktails. In your elated state you decide to video your friends/family at play with your state of the art camcorder. Sadly the steadiness of your hand is impaired by a decreased blood/alcohol ratio. Fuzzy logic comes to the rescue. The camcorder recognises that the people being filmed generally do not

shake. And even if they do, they do not shake at the same frequency as everything else in the picture. Consequently the camcorder corrects your shaking. This is a non-trivial piece of processing.

❏ Neural networks – By building a conceptual picture based on information gleaned to date, this technology is then able to anticipate/predict the outcome for a given set of circumstances. This is very useful to meteorologists, those involved in exploratory mining and gamblers in general.

So AI has come on a pace, but 5GLs haven't. From a commercial point of view they are irrelevant and a big disappointment. There is nothing to suggest a resurgence in 5GLs, though the momentum building up in respect of nano-technology (see chapter 11) could change that.

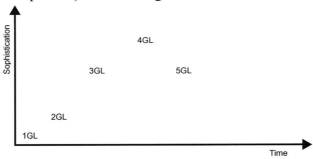

5.11 Evolution of Programming Languages

Pseudocode

You might from time to time hear of psuedocode, particularly if you work closely with programmers or ate in a lot of Silicon Valley restaurants. In a good market you would be overhearing the diners. In a bad market you would be overhearing the table staff. Back to the plot. This is not another programming language or even generation of language. It is in fact a technique used by programmers prior to programming.

Pseudocode is a bit like the notes you made prior to giving a speech to remind you of what to say, but not necessarily how to say it. Before programmers, particularly those involved in business logic programming, write the software they think through and document what they have to write. Decoupling 'the what' from 'the how' helps programmers think more lucidly.

Pseudocode is language independent. There is no internationally agreed standard but many organizations have their own guidelines. Generally speaking good pseudocode should be understandable to people with no specific background in the language in which the software will be coded.

Pseudocode competes with flow-charts as a design technique for programmers. Flowcharts are more visible but require the investment of a drawing tool and are more time consuming to produce. Pseudocode requires nothing more than a text editor.

If you ever attend a function where the main speaker is of a technical orientation, ask politely to take a look at their speech notes. You'll understand what I mean. Here's an example:

For all wedding receptions where speaker is best man
    Introduce oneself
    Reveal embarrassing story about the groom
    If story is well received then
        Tell another 5 such stories
    Else
        Pretend to be drunk
        Mumble something about the speech being tampered with
    Make flattering comments about the happy couple
    Make appropriate toasts
    End speech
End speech making at wedding receptions in general.

5.12 An everyday example of pseudocode

Purists would argue that the logic lacks structure. Just ignore them.

Summary

As you can see the world of programming languages is a relatively complex one. You are strongly advised to get to grips with this area, as they are a key component of application development. Applications are the key element of IT. Consequently programming languages are key to the IT industry.

Databases

Overview

A database in general terms is a storage mechanism for data. This makes your diary and address book both databases.

A database has some form of filing or ordering of data. Typically diaries order data chronologically and address book alphabetically by first or second name (The lack of an international standard on this front has caused diplomatic rifts in my own household).

Shopping lists ordered by shop and even sub ordered by aisle are databases, and so the 'list' goes on.

The point of this rambling introduction is to make the point that databases in the computing sense are no different to the databases that we have been using for centuries. The difference being that they are electronically based.

Think of computer based databases as electronic filing cabinets. The labels on the pockets and drawers are determined by the database developer, whose job it is to develop the data management layer of the application. So when an IT department or software house needs to build an application they will need to purchase what is in effect an empty electronic filing cabinet.

The application will determine how the pockets and drawers are labelled. So for an investment bank trading system the drawers may have labels such as trade, account and customer. Within each drawer there will be pockets labelled trade date, account number and customer email address.

5.13 e-Filing cabinet

CRUD

The key reasons for having a database are to:
- Create new data
- Read data
- Update data
- Delete data.

CRUD for short. Alternatively you can remember this as Create, Read, Amend and Purge. This mnemonic is equally squalid.

To give this a real world setting, let us take two everyday examples:
- Create new data
  - You get a new friend so you add them to your address book
  - A plane comes into your airspace, they are added to the air traffic database
- Read data
  - From time to time you need to phone them or write to them so you look up their details in your address book
  - A curious air traffic controller notes that the plane is shown as a red icon on the screen and clicks on it to ascertain more details

- ❏ Update data
  - o Your friend moves and so you update their details in your address book
  - o The air traffic controller is concerned and updates the details to reflect that the plane may be hostile
- ❏ Delete data.
  - o Your friend runs off with your partner and so you remove their data from your address book
  - o Three tenths of a second later the air traffic control database has one less record

No matter how sophisticated the application, the underlying database performs fundamentally the same operations.

Engine

When one purchases a 'build your own' database kit from Oracle or Microsoft, not only are you getting the construction tools but also the engine that will enable the database to function when the application is up and running.

This engine is essentially software that manages the data passing into and out of the database. It's all very well building a database, but without the engine you will not be able to use it. Fortunately all database development packages provide this engine.

Database types

Not only are there many database products in the market place, there are many types of database. In the same way that there are many cook books on the market, there are also many different cooking categories, cordon bleu, barbecue, vegetarian and so on.

I'll take this opportunity to present you with a brief history of databases.

For the first few million years people used their brains to store information. These were typically real-time in nature, as any delays in processing the positional data of a sabre tooth tiger could prove fatal.

In the last few thousand years etchings in stone and wood created the market for persistent storage, that is to say storage that was retained so as to be available some time in the future. Papyrus and paper joined the product range latterly. Memory reuse was an issue though.

With the arrival of computing, data could be stored mechanically and eventually electronically. Looking into the future, data will be stored photonically and quantumally.

It was only with the arrival of computers did the issue of how the data would be stored become an issue. The original databases were called flat files. These were a bit like typing your diary into a word processor one line per day where the first 8 characters had the format dd/mm/yy or some such format followed by a space and then a string of characters that comprised the entry for the associated day.

This diary has the advantage of being in a natural chronological order, but what if you wanted to look at all the entries for the first day of every month. This would be possible but very time consuming as the user would have to hop over irrelevant records.

So the concept of indexed files was introduced. This speeded up the searching process as the key data types of the database, for example, employee name, date of trade, postcode were individually indexed.

But stuffing all the data into one file was inefficient. What if the database held purchases associated with customers? With one file each record would have to repeat the customers personal details every time a new purchase was made. This was a major overhead in terms of storage and speed of retrieval.

Relational databases

Today we have relational databases. You might hear of hierarchical and networked databases, but these are essentially legacy technologies. IBM created the relational concept in the seventies. In fact the person responsible is known as Dr Ted Codd, who is revered in database circles.

The relational database was underpinned by mathematical rigor, being based on Set Theory. By separating out repeating data, such as a customer's personal details and putting them in a separate file (where the customer's details were only recorded once) and then linking this file back to the orders using some identifier such as customer number, Dr Codd had found an effective way to significantly reduce the database's storage footprint. This was seen as excellent news given that in the seventies storage retailed at about £2 million per megabyte.

Relational databases dominate the market today. Some of the popular names include:

- ❏ Oracle
- ❏ SQL Server
- ❏ Access
- ❏ DB2
- ❏ Adabas.

Others that were once stars include:

- ❏ Informix
- ❏ Ingres
- ❏ Sybase
- ❏ Paradox
- ❏ Progress
- ❏ dBase
  - o Including Foxpro and Clipper

5.14. Examples of relational databases

Despite their popularity, relational databases are based on seventies technology. Data storage was limited to numbers, dates, strings (ie characters, eg. "Hello") and Booleans (True or False).

In the late eighties a need emerged to store 'non standard' data such as photos and eventually video. In response to this the object oriented database market was created. OO databases could in theory store anything even thoughts and smells. There was no limit.

The OO database market was full of wide-eyed technology entrepreneurs. Unlike the recent dotcommers, these people had business plans and genuine technology to offer. However their look and feel was a little more Human League / Joy Division than today's Silicon Valley look. They planned to topple the world of relational technology.

Regrettably perhaps, the established giants crushed the upstarts. The relational vendors tried to 'cludge' this new OO technology onto their existing products. The first wave of offerings was dismal. Today the OODB upstarts are no more and the relational vendors remain dominant.

Thus the relational offerings today have rather confused technology under the bonnet. Analogy wise, putting complex data such as video into a relational database is much the same as having to dismantle your car when you want to put it in the garage. Admittedly dismantling is not your responsibility, but there is both a processing and time overhead. At some point today's database vendors will need to go back to the drawing board.

Having said that, database technology is essentially a commodity and so there would probably be very little additional return for what would be a large investment. So this is unlikely to happen anytime soon.

Post relational

Relational technology solved a big problem several decades ago when it reduced the amount of storage required to hold a given amount of data. The price paid for this was in data accessibility. Today getting meaningful data out of a relational database is like 'pulling a tooth'.

This has spawned what are loosely called post relational databases. These databases are optimised for querying rather than storage. Strictly speaking this technology has become a database 'bolt on' rather than a database successor. You will hear terms such as:

- OLAP – Online analytical processer
    - And even ROLAP and MOLAP
        - Rollmops are something quite different
- Data mining
- Business analytics.

None of these are new concepts, but they do represent one of the few growth areas in the world of data storage.

SQL

It would be rude to talk about databases and not introduce you to SQL, or Structured Query Language. To affect the air of a seasoned techie pronounce it SeQueL. To affect the air of someone whose sole IT education is based on taking a thirty year old university textbook out of the local library pronounce it SQuirreL.

It is a language, but not a good one, as it doesn't support programming constructs such as decision-making. It does more than querying, which implies reading the data only. Think CRUD. And it is far from structured. Ask a hardened database developer to show you their most impressive line of squirrel, sorry sequel, and you'll see what I mean. So the name is misleading.

Think of sequel as a database access language that enables the user to perform CRUD operations. NB. Users do not write sequel, it gets generated behind the scene and is then fired off to the database engine for processing.

Important facts about sequel:

- ❏ It was developed for relational databases and can be loosely used as an indicator of whether a database is relational. If the database is using sequel it is very likely to be a relational database (often written RDBMS – the MS being Management System)
- ❏ It is an international standard. Nobody owns it. IBM created it and handed over control to ISO, the standards body to the planet Earth
- ❏ Microsoft does not own it, despite the name being woven into their popular database product
- ❏ All RDBMS vendors offer their own variant of it
    - o Each adhering to the standard more or less, but adding their own extended features that are designed to lock the customer into the database product
- ❏ All database developers are comfortable writing sequel. So should all competent DBAs (DataBase Administrators). You might fancy trying

your own hand at this. If you have access to MS Access, try creating a new query using the query-building tool, which automatically generates the associated sequel. DO seek permission from your DBA before attempting this.

Summary

Data is the lifeblood of an organization. How it is stored will determine how accessible it is to the users and thus how effectively it can be put to work for the benefit of the organization.

Database development tools are thus critical to the development of applications.

Modern databases are generally underpinned by ancient technology. This is an issue, but not necessarily a critical one.

In summary

This chapter has focused on application development technologies

- ❏ The application can be subdivided into the:
  - o User interface
  - o Business logic
  - o Data management
- ❏ Programming languages enable us to develop the user interface and the business logic
- ❏ Databases provide the means to manage the data
- ❏ The real value of IT to business lies in the quality of the applications and so application development lies at the heart of the IT industry.

Test yourself?

19. The user interface

    a. Expert programmers recognise the benefits of having light green text on dark green backgrounds

    b. Is confined to the technologies the user can touch, such as the mouse, chair and keyboard

    c. Is too overrated. Real programmers focus on the business logic

    d. Users should really make more effort to appreciate it when programmers produce 'clever interfaces'

20. Programming languages

    a. Are the instructions that make the hardware do things

    b. Are the tools that enable programmers to write the instructions that make the hardware do things

    c. Are not used to build operating systems

    d. Machine code remains very popular in some industries.

21. Databases

    a. Are only used with a minority of applications

    b. OO databases are the most commonly used today

    c. Dr Codd is the founder of the RDBMS

    d. Are used to develop the business logic layer of the application.

22. SQL

    a. Was created and is owned by Microsoft

    b. Is very closely associated with RDBMSs

    c. Is a necessary skill for 21st century users to have

    d. Those 'in the know' pronounce it squirrel.

23. Java

    a. Is one of the most popular databases in the market

    b. Was created by Sun Microsystems

    c. In the future your fridge could be Java enabled

    d. Is so named because it enables the programmer to break the application down into little Indonesian-like islands.

Section 3

Architectures
How IT systems hang together

Here we see how technology has evolved from the original mainframes and dumb terminals right through to what we have today and beyond. In effect we are covering IT architectures.

Chapter 6

Carbon Dating the IT Investment

Why read this? Computing has changed considerably from the dawn of the IT industry. This chapter details how technology has evolved from an architectural perspective. By reading this chapter you will be better placed to 'carbon date' the technology architectures you encounter.

In the beginning..

The first ever computer, Mark 1, was built by Harvard University in the 1940s. Other names that can be used to ingratiate oneself with tech sector doyens include Eniac and Univac. In the UK Station X at Bletchley Park is discussed with much affection, as is the enigmatic Alan Turing.

In the 1960s IBM established itself as a leader in the commercial computing marketplace. Other players included Rand, Sperry, Boroughs and NCR.

IT's roots began in the 19th century, evolving from mechanical tabulators to vacuum tubes and transistors and on into solid-state technology. In the days of mechanical computing, when a system was said to have bugs, these were in fact real insects that were clogging up the machinery.

IBM, which has contributed greatly to the evolution of IT, did not recognise its true potential. In 1943, its chairman Thomas Watson decreed that there was a world market for probably five computers at most. This set the standard ever since in respect of accurate IT market forecasting.

Mainframe

Defined

The first commercial computers were referred to as mainframes. They were physically massive devices that could have a footprint greater than a tennis court. Consequently they were very expensive and so were affordable only to organizations that had a real need to computerize their operations, eg. Governments and the Finance Sector.

Dumb Terminals

Remember that mainframes existed before the PC, and so users accessed these monolithic computers by what are known as dumb terminals, sometimes unaffectionately known as 'green screens'.

In many respects a dumb terminal looks like a PC. It had a monitor and keyboard, but lacked the modern 'pizza box', which holds the processor and hard disk. This lack of processing and memory capacity made dumb terminal an apt name.

Dumb terminals, unlike PCs:

- Could not store files
- Did not have an intuitive iconic GUI (Graphical User Interface). Instead they were limited to displaying characters
- Did not do any processing. This took place on the mainframe.

This last point is critical. The lack of processing power at the 'front end' meant that dumb terminals were invariably slow. Screen updates had to be downloaded from the mainframe, leading to perceptible delays for the user.

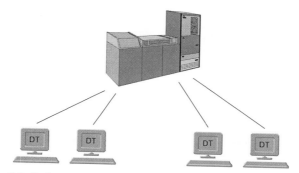

6.1 Schematic of a mainframe architecture

Centralised architecture

This model of computing, whereby all the processing took place on one 'box' is referred to as a centralised architecture. We will soon see that this approach is no longer in vogue.

NB. Storage was also centralised onto the mainframe. So the dumb terminal was also a storage-free device. From an architectural perspective it is the processing aspect that is most significant. But keep in mind that today storage is racing back onto the 'radar screen' of IT management.

IT Department perspective

For the IT department, this was the golden era of computing. All the power was behind the IT fence. Users could only cause limited damage to dumb terminals, unlike PCs today. In fact when I first used IT, I had to go into an air-conditioned terminal room, which had the feel of an intergalactic convicts transporter. 'Chained' to the terminal, any sightings of food being munched or fizzy drinks being slurped was an invitation to be shot. If you wanted to print a document, the request was submitted in writing, and if the IT department staff were in a good mood you would get the printout the following day.

Those 'halcyon days' are over, but there is a gravitational pull back to this model, as we will soon learn.

The PC era

Defined

Today a PC (Personal Computer) is regarded as a single user device based on IBM's original 'open' specification. The key characteristics being that:

- ❏ The processor is either made by Intel or copied from Intel's specification
- ❏ The operating system is Microsoft Windows.

The latter characteristic is slightly under threat as some PC vendors dip their toe into the world of Linux. Time will tell as to whether this is the first sign that Microsoft is losing its grip on the PC marketplace.

Apple users will have a view on the above definition, as perhaps will Atari, Sinclair and Commodore64 owners. These are also PCs in the traditional sense, but the dominance of IBM's specification in the commercial and governmental marketplace has effectively redefined the term.

Possibly IBM could be credited with being one of the first organizations to adopt the open source model. By making their PC specification open to anyone who wanted to clone it, IBM effectively enlisted the help of other manufacturers in growing the PC marketplace. The move gave birth to Dell and Gateway amongst others.

Over the years only the Apple range of computers (for usability) and Sun workstations (for power) have posed a threat to the IBM spec PC. Some of the CAD (Computer Aided Design) vendors developed their own desktops with powerful graphical processing capability. But today the IBM spec PC has caught up and overtaken these contenders.

Again Apple users will have a view on this and a justifiable one at that. Unfortunately Apple's marketing, which oozes creativity, did not resonate with the traditional world of business and thus Apple has been consigned to the commercial periphery. That said, it is making a gentle comeback in the server marketplace, and not just because it offers a range of pastel shades.

So from this point onwards any mention of PC is a direct reference to the IBM spec PC.

Mini mainframes

The arrival of the PC was a revolution for corporations. Users felt very empowered by the fact that they had their own processing power and memory storage on their desk. Architecturally they had a desktop mainframe at their disposal.

The early PCs occupied a rather large footprint on the desktop. The 'electron gun' monitor was a contributor to this. The 5¼" floppy disk drive and the internal disk drive also contributed to the high desktop real estate occupancy.

The hard disk tapped to what sounded like a precursor to 'Lord of the Dance' and the printer had to be housed in a soundproof cover. Possibly the cover was also bullet proof given the user frustrations associated with dot matrix printing onto a cartwheel driven paper feeder). Nonetheless the arrival of the PC was a major step forward.

From CUI to GUI

The first generation of PC's looked very much like dumb terminals. Whilst they were limited to displaying characters (CUI – Character User Interface), they were able to extend the spectrum capability beyond the colour green.

Multitasking was not an option with the first PCs. Today we happily 'ALT TAB' our way through the day as we flit from email to web to word processor. Back then you ran one application at a time. Flitting between applications was an option reserved only for the ultra-patient.

DOS (see chapter 3) as an operating system, had its limitations, but it did make the computer just about usable (by technologists). NB. There were superior variants of MS DOS in the marketplace, most notably DR-DOS. But it is marketing that counts and so Microsoft took charge of the PC.

Eventually Microsoft enhanced the PC experience by introducing Windows, which offered a GUI (Graphical User Interface) 'look and feel'. Windows 95 was the first version that was generally acceptable to business users.

Enhancements to memory management made multitasking an option, which ensured from that point onwards no email was too trivial to divert our attention away from the task at hand.

Centralised architecture

It is worth re-emphasising that the PC constituted a centralised architecture in that the user's applications ran on the desktop. Unlike the mainframe, there was typically more than one PC in the organization. Each PC constituted an 'island of computing'. Unfortunately these islands were remote and so sharing of resources and co-working was difficult. Early solutions to networking included sneakernet. Ask anyone over forty to explain the mechanics of this. It will bring a smile to their face.

6.2 Another centralised architecture

IT Department perspective

The PC in many respects represented the first ever computer virus. All of a sudden a department went from one PC in the corner to one per user. Every user represented the enemy. The new IT department perspective was that users broke things and the IT department fixed them. This was not an unreasonable position to take, as PCs were (and are) not very robust from the user's perspective.

'PC experts' in the user community felt obliged to demonstrate their prowess to lesser mortals, and thus inadvertently helped spread such practices as 'clearing the hard disk'. The software did not help. The <CTRL+C> key press combination in one application caused a file to be copied; in another it cleared the hard disk. Thus users had to either remember the shortcut key combinations or carry around strips of cardboard, which when overlaid onto the keyboard would detail the associated functionality of the keyboard in the context of the application being used. These portable 'key press solutions' were very popular in the 80s. Microsoft, in its defence, has played a very positive role in standardising the user experience ("....and that is why we should remain a monopoly, your honour").

Software license management was impossible. "How many copies are we using?" "What versions of the software are we using?" Data management (backing up and archiving) was literally impossible, thus leaving the IT department exposed.

The PC liberated the users but dissolved the IT department's power-base. Possibly the PC has been the greatest contributor to business-IT tensions.

The networking era

The Rationale

Both the IT department and the business recognised that having isolated islands of computing was having an impact on productivity. For example, some smart user might have developed a customer database that needed to be accessible to other users. Queuing up to access the PC on which the database resided, whilst the smart user had lunch or was in a meeting, was not recognised as an optimal resource-sharing model. Something had to be done about it.

What is a network?

This spawned the concept of the network. A network is a collection of computing devices that are linked together using some form of communication technology. Thus computers on the network could now share resources such as files and printers.

The networking technology comprised:

- ❑ The cable, which linked the computing devices together
- ❑ The Network Interface Device (aka NIA – Network Interface Adapter), which enabled the computing device to be linked to the cable.

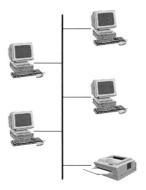

6.3 A network

The original technology for cabling was that used for telephony, ie twisted pair cabling. This is still in use today. NB. The computer network, despite its cabling heritage, could only handle data, and not voice. Thus the dawn of computer-telephony integration (CTI) was some way off.

Today the cabling options extend to:

❑ Coaxial

❑ Fibre

❑ Wireless

6.4 Cabling options

As networks grew more sophisticated, the requirement for bridging devices emerged, ie technologies that linked networks together. Thus you may well hear of the following:

❑ Bridge	❑ Gateway
❑ Router	❑ Firewall
❑ Brouter	❑ Switch
❑ Hub	

6.4 Internetworking options

Key terms

Other key terms you may encounter are:

- ❏ LAN – Local Area Network
  - ○ These link computing devices together on one network
- ❏ MAN – Metropolitan Area Network
  - ○ Simply a LAN that spans a town/city
- ❏ CAN – Campus Area Network
  - ○ Simply a LAN that spans a campus or business park
- ❏ WAN – Wide Area Network
  - ○ This is a network that links LANs together, typically over large distances
- ❏ SAN – Satellite Area Network
  - ○ A wireless variant of a WAN, where the connection points are located in outer space
- ❏ SAN – Storage Area Network
  - ○ A high speed network dedicated to data storage devices
- ❏ VAN – Value Added Network
  - ○ A service provided by a third party that includes network connectivity plus additional services, eg. security
- ❏ VPN – Virtual Private Network
  - ○ A secure network that operates over a public network (most typically the Internet)
- ❏ Van the Man
  - ○ An aging Belfast rock star, who has very little to do with networking and IT in general.

6.5 Networking terms

127

The file server era

The Rationale

The ability to share information was a major step forward architecturally. The original networks worked on a master-slave architecture, ie. there was one computer that in effect told the others what to do. This model had the benefit of centralised control, but failed to exploit the intelligence of the slave computers.

Eventually the master-slave model was replaced by what was then known as peer-to-peer networking. The title rightly suggests that all computers on the network are equal. However the question arose as to where common files should be stored. Up until then shared files were randomly sprinkled across the network. If user A at PC A created a file to be shared, it resided on A's PC and so on. This made finding files a challenge and data backup a nightmare.

Thus someone had the bright idea of putting the shared files on one computer. This computer was unlike the others in that it needed:

- ❏ More disk storage
- ❏ To cope with multiple users
- ❏ More power to cope with multiple users.

Consequently this computer was different to the other computers. One might say that it provided a service to the other computers, or at least their users. Thus the term server was coined.

These early servers were used to share files and to share the printer, which was attached directly to the server. The size of the server was roughly proportional to the number of users.

Users had no reason to directly interact with the server, and so it was kept out of their reach (in the IT department). They accessed the server via their own desktops via the network.

6.6 The arrival of the file server

The client-server era

Extending the server's role

It is important to recognise the difference between networked computing and distributed computing. The former is designed with storage in mind. The latter is designed with processing in mind.

Up until now the server was used as a file storage device. The next natural step was to utilise its processing power to share some of the load associated with the user applications.

The distributed computing refers to an architecture whereby the processing of one or more applications is shared amongst more than one computer. This is unlike the previous file server architecture, where the application simply ran on one machine, eg. the Word processor on the PC.

The following section on client server will bring this to life.

Client-server defined

In the early nineties, client-server was the big theme in selling applications. The ability to enable multiple users to concurrently run an application without fear that the associated data would somehow get corrupted or overwritten was very attractive.

Essentially client-server is an architecture whereby an application is split across two computers, typically the desktop and the server. Think of any application that is used simultaneously by two or more users, and you are thinking of a client server application.

Examples include:

- Trading systems
- HR systems
- Customer relationship management systems

Each of these systems has the following in common:

- The database resides on the server (data management)
- The software by which the user accesses the database runs on the desktop (user interface)
- The clever part of the application that does the processing resides either on the desktop or the server or indeed divided across both. For example the bit within the insurance quotation system that calculates the insurance premium based on the data supplied by the user. (business logic)

Client-server applications are multi-user applications and so Word and Excel cannot be considered client-server. They are single user desktop applications.

See chapter 4 for more on applications.

An application vendor today pitching client-server as an impressive feature would be like a car dealer enthusing about the fact that she sells cars with brakes.

Prior to client-server, architectures could be thought of in purely hardware terms. The client–server architecture should be thought of as a software architecture, and more specifically an application architecture.

6.7 Client-server – A decentralised architecture

Server

Server in this context means the software end of the application that provides a service. This is distinct from the server we know to be hardware. In most cases the server software sits on the server hardware and for many people this distinction is academic. But beware, servers come in the form of hardware and software and this can cause confusion if you simply associate the word server with hardware.

Client

It is also worth pointing out now that the client in client-server is also software. It requests services from the server and so conceptually is a client (or customer) of the server. People also talk about client devices, most typically user/front-end devices. Again there is a difference between client hardware and client software. And yet again the fact that in most cases the client software resides on client hardware renders this an imperceptible difference for most people.

Some people think the client in client-server is a reference to the user. Again it is not. It is a reference to the software that barks orders at the server software.

Client-server is not the easiest of concepts to grasp, but if you appreciate that it is the corner stone of distributed computing and involves splitting the application across two platforms, then you know enough to make sense of the world of IT architectures.

Thick-client

As client-server grew in popularity so did the amount of processing at the desktop end. This suited Intel and Microsoft. The applications became more client-heavy with respect to processing. It became standard to replace one's PC every 12 to 18 months.

This evolving model was known as thick or fat client computing. The 'Wintel axis' was a term used to acknowledge how this client-server variant favoured both Microsoft and Intel.

Users found themselves with increasingly powerful desktop machines, which led to greater management and maintenance problems for the IT department. For the brighter criminal, stealing a PC was worth more than its resale value. This architecture invariably meant that users could accidentally or otherwise leave corporate files on the PC's hard disk. Such files would have real value in the right (ie. wrong) hands.

Thin-client

The thin-client architecture emerged as a backlash to thick-client. The main thrust of the thin-client revolution was the need to reduce the total cost of ownership of the desktop, which included not just the purchase price but also the in-service costs. Other drivers included:

- ❏ Security
- ❏ Licence management
- ❏ User control
- ❏ Data management

Oracle was one of the first organizations to introduce the concept of the thin-client architecture (known then as the Network Computer). It proposed a computer that looked much like a PC, but there were some fundamental differences. Specifically it had:

- ❏ No hard disk
- ❏ Very little processing power
- ❏ No storage media drives (eg. CD drive)

The thin-client architecture presumed that all data and software resided on the server. When the user invoked an application, the client component was downloaded onto the thin-client device, and was used as per the thick-client model. (I have used the term device to highlight the fact that the technology through which the user accesses the application is not necessarily a traditional computer.) Any data files associated with the running of the application would be stored on the server.

This model is very attractive to the IT department. It essentially brought the architecture wheel full circle; only this time around the 'dumb terminal' was graphical and had some processing power. The frequent desktop upgrade cycle was over and control of IT was back behind the IT department fence, its rightful home, some would say.

Thin-client as a concept has been around for years. Oracle was a little too ahead of its time. Microsoft has adapted its strategy to embrace thin-client as a hedge bet against the demise of the PC.

The market reality today is that most of us have thick-client. Quite a few have migrated to thin-client, either in part or in a pseudo thin-manner, ie. whipping out the hard disk and media drives from their standard PCs.

Thin has its down side, not least through the increased burden it puts on the network as users download the client element of their applications.

The early 21st century downturn in technology spend has put the migration to thin-client on hold. And as we will see in the next chapter there are some imaginative alternatives to thin-client being touted.

Outsourcing Today

Outsourcing can be thought of as an architectural option. Unlike other architectures we have talked about or will talk about it does not presume a particular technology configuration.

However the option for the IT department to be managed by a third party is significant to the role of the IT department.

Outsourcing in an IT sense is handing over the management of your IT, applications, data and infrastructure to a third party. Most likely this will involve handing over the organization's existing IT assets, including the IT staff.

To enjoy the economies of scale, the outsourcing company may choose to deliver IT services using it own technology at its own site. But sometimes the outsourcer simply takes over the running of the IT department and remains camped on their client's site.

Outsourcing contracts tend to:

- Involve a transfer of employment from the client to the outsourcing company

- ❑ Involve redundancies as the outsourcing company sifts out the 'dead wood' and sometimes even 'live wood' to ensure that the newly acquired technology infrastructure is run as efficiently (some might say adequately) as possible
- ❑ Involve a significant upfront investment on the part of the outsourcing company
  - o On the understanding that it is getting a contract sufficiently long and large to get payback (and some)
- ❑ Include specifics in respect of service levels
  - o These can be used to measure whether the outsourcing company is actually delivering.

Outsourcing may appear to be the business to be in. Large monetary value and cash flow for several years, but the bigger the contract, the bigger the risk to both parties.

Outsourcing can be thought of as trusting the organization's 'nervous system' to a third party. The supplier's failure to deliver will have a profound impact on the business. The outsourcing company needs to establish whether the client will remain a going concern for the duration of the contract. From the supplier's perspective, significant upfront investment coupled with a liquidated client is a sure way to make a negative dent in one's cash flow. Ask outsourcing giant EDS.

IT offers no competitive advantage

Outsourcing to some extent treats IT as a commodity that offers no competitive advantage and consequently the focus should be on driving down its cost. Smart organizations recognise that, whilst some elements of IT are indeed commodities, there is real competitive advantage to be gained through applications that:

- ❑ Harness the knowledge within the organization
- ❑ Help in business decision-making
- ❑ Provide customers with innovative offerings

It is not clear how this is woven into a service-level agreement.

Keep in mind that it is possible to outsource the infrastructure but retain control of the applications, and vice versa. The former is more likely to result in an organization successfully differentiating itself through the innovative use of technology.

In Summary

- ❑ IT has come a long way in the last 60 years
- ❑ Where the storage and processing takes place has changed over this period
- ❑ As far as the IT department is concerned, despite the benefits of standardisation and a GUI interface, the PC has been bad for business
- ❑ Despite this pressure from the IT department, the PC may continue to flourish. That depends on who prevails in selling their vision of the next generation of IT architectures. All will be revealed in the next chapter.

Test Yourself

24. Mainframes:

    a. Are another term used to describe a handheld computer

    b. Were designed with PCs in mind

    c. Were designed with dumb terminals in mind

    d. The older mainframes have been converted from gas fuelled to electricity.

25. The advantages of thin-client include:

    a. Improved security

    b. Improved licence management

    c. Reduced burden on the network

    d. Less expensive at lunchtime.

26. Outsourcing:
   a. Can be very profitable for the outsourcing company
   b. Involves the applications only
   c. Involves the databases and hardware only
   d. Can be a useful technique for thinning out the IT department.

27. The PC:
   a. Is a source of much delight to the IT department
   b. Is mostly associated with thick-client computing
   c. Was invented by Microsoft
   d. Was invented by Apple.

28. The IT department:
   a. Will soon be history
   b. Is attracted to thin-client computing
   c. Are always impressed when users choose to configure their own PCs
   d. Recognises that networking is much more than swapping business cards at cocktail parties.

Chapter 7

21st Century Systems

Why read this? Anticipating trends leads to competitive advantage. This chapter lays out the most high profile options for IT architectures going forward.

Grid computing

Grid computing defined

The concept of the grid originated in the academic arena. In the same manner in which the US Department of Defense spawned the Internet, academic institutions have laid the foundations for what is now called grid computing.

Their model comprised hugely powerful servers linked together by high-speed networks. There is nothing remarkable about that. The clever bit is how the resources are used. Architecturally the network of servers behaves as one supercomputer. Thus a scientist simulating atomic collisions treats the grid as one computer. Where his application runs is academic, even to him. In fact subject to the resources available on the grid, his application may be partitioned across a number of computers.

As Sun Microsystems stated many years ago "The network is the computer" and that is very much the case for grid computing. Think of grid computing as an architecture that makes optimum use of one's computing resources.

Rationale

IBM has taken this concept to market, with the help of a number of niche suppliers. The argument for grid computing is compelling.

If you had to guess what the utilisation is of your PC, not the percentage of hours in which it is used, but the percentage usage of the processor's capacity, what would you say?

Well a book can only be so interactive, so I'll tell you the answer. It's under 10%. Similarly servers have a utilisation of circa 20%. Thus every organization that has an investment in IT has not only spent money on fast depreciating assets, but is dramatically failing to get good value from them.

In steps IBM and co. with a solution that in effect pools an organization's unused IT assets. When a user is 'happily' typing a report, their PC could also be running part of the company's payroll programme. Think of this as a virtual server.

Thus every 'client' device can also behave like a 'server', providing a service to client software resident elsewhere. This model was previously known as P2P (peer-to-peer). Some may even refer to it as server-server, a variant on client-server (See Chapter 6).

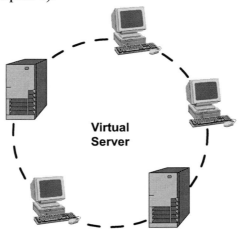

Virtual
Server

7.1 The Grid Computing model

Impact on IT department

Whilst the business case is compelling, the underlying technology is terrifyingly complex. Worse still, the PC continues to play a role in the architecture. What's more there will be an upward pressure to buy more powerful PCs to help in balancing the processing load across the organization's network.

This will perpetuate the problems mentioned in the last chapter such as security, data management and user control.

There will be tremendous pressure to adopt this model, as it seems like a solution modelled for these money/value conscious times and so will be very attractive to CFOs.

Impact on business

Business people have always had a lingering suspicion that the IT department exists to keep itself in business. Thus delivering better value is low down their 'to do' list.

The reality is that some IT departments are very conscious of delivering value and for some the concept of value is a nicety to dwell on when on vacation, where they aren't bogged down in simply keeping the system available for the users.

Thus grid computing looks like a technology solution packaged to solve a business problem. (Technology marketers appear to be getting better at positioning their products.) Thus businesses can relate to this and so are likely to push hard for its deployment.

Much evangelising needs to be done before this becomes an option that is well understood in the business community. IBM recognises that. It has the resources to drive this model to the centre of the business radar.

Utility computing

Utility computing defined

Like grid computing, utility computing is quite a compelling vision. But even more so than grid computing, utility computing is a leap of faith.

Again IBM is leading the way in promoting this model. The vision is that IT is nothing more than a utility in the same manner as water, electricity and telecoms. As a user you treat it as a service and only pay for what you use.

In some ways this can be seen as outsourcing, but there are differences:

- ❑ With utility computing you only pay for what you use
- ❑ The utility model can be used in-house. So the IT department could use this model to allocate resources to different IT projects. The utility model coupled with grid computing could thus provide much better resource management.
- ❑ Outsourcing in an IT sense involves handing over all or a significant aspect of your IT to a third party for a fixed fee. Utility computing is more like the data bureaux of days gone by, whereby organizations contract a third party to take care of processing some aspect of their business, eg. pay-roll.

At a fundamental level, utility computing can be as simple as providing computing power and storage, with the supplier taking no responsibility for the applications.

Rationale

The concept of technology-on-tap will have appeal for organizations that need access to computing power on an 'as and when' basis. The decision to go down the utility computing route will need to be weighed up against having one's own infrastructure.

The utility model suggests that IT is a commodity that provides little value, in much the same manner as electricity. So why try to create your own electricity in-house?

Certainly data storage and processing power are commodities. At a business application level, the term commodity applies only if all the applications used are standard packages.

However if utility computing takes off at the application (data bureau) level, this could coincide nicely with the emergence of Business Process Outsourcing, and thus become mainstream pretty quickly. BPO by the way is a variant on outsourcing that is oriented towards solving a business problem using technology, as opposed to solving a technology problem using technology (traditional outsourcing).

7.2 Utility Computing

Impact on IT department

IT could look at utility computing as a model to better manage resources. There is no idle-time/utilisation issue with a 'pay as you go' model. The IT department, if sufficiently large, could create its own utility model using the existing investment of in-house servers and storage devices.

It could then charge each IT project in proportion to its resource usage. In fact it could go one step further than using the utility model as a way of allocating resources within the IT department and actually turn the IT department into a utility to the business.

Thus businesses users, or more specifically departments, could be charged based on usage. This would certainly focus the IT department into meeting the needs of the business and focus the business into getting best value from the IT department.

In any case the underlying technology to make this happen will be non-trivial. A migration to either an in-house or out-house variant of utility computing will constitute a major project that may well divert limited resources away from servicing the business's needs today.

This may warrant asking the business to provide more IT resources. Only a forward thinking CFO will see the sense in this.

Impact on business

Given the generally poor return associated with IT assets, particularly hardware, the utility model offers a potentially boardroom-pleasing solution. The upside of this variable-price model is that you only pay for what you use. The downside of a variable-price model is that the anticipated spend may be wildly inaccurate.

As mentioned the migration to utility computing will not be a 'plug and go' exercise. The initial upfront investment may well make this a non-starter.

Web services

Web services defined

Web-services is a term coined to capture the act of serving up applications to the users via the web. What we have traditionally known as applications are now being referred to as services.

Why the word change? Applications imply capital outlay. You buy Microsoft Office as a capital investment, usually with the investment upfront. Services on the other hand imply cash flow. You use, you pay. Software houses are looking towards a model that will enable them to get more money from the customers, so a move from a capital expenditure model of payment to a cash flow model is attractive.

The original name for web services was Application Service Provision (ASP). This model involves delivering applications to the users via the web. It can be deployed either by the IT department or a third party. So what was once called ASP is increasingly referred to as web services.

The dream is to have a world where applications are broken down into their basic components. Let's take a word processor as an example. In the future this will be a software suite comprising spell checker, grammar checker, editor and so on. Rather than each word processor vendor create their own 'bundled' spell checker, they may call upon the spell checker service provided by another vendor. The user is oblivious to this. They believe they are using a word processor delivered by a particular vendor. The reality could be that the word processor is made up of 'components' from a number of vendors that have mutually agreed a pricing model. The cross vendor charging is invisible to the user.

These objects reside on different parts of the World Wide Web. Thus standardisation is required in terms of:

❑ Communication

❑ Security

❑ Payment

The big vendors are currently wrestling to have their vision of web services become the prevailing vision. Microsoft's dotnet model is most high profile. Sun Microsystems's J2EE is the main rival. Companies such as IBM, BEA Systems and Oracle are also jostling for dominance.

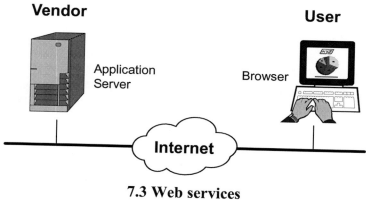

7.3 Web services

Rationale

Web-services is very attractive to both the user and the supplier.

The user benefits as follows:

- ❏ Web-services enables organizations to in effect outsource their applications
- ❏ There is no great capital outlay
    - o Although ultimately the user may part with more money
- ❏ No more repurchasing of software upgrades. Users get the (perhaps dubious) 'benefit' of always having access to the latest version of the software
- ❏ Support becomes part of the service, rather than something that comes to an end after a set period.

The vendor benefits as follows:

- ❏ Access to wider markets. 'Big ticket' applications, eg the deployment of an ERP system, could only be sold to substantial enterprises with 'deep pockets'. Deploying a standardised version of the software via the web will enable the vendor to access smaller organizations anywhere in the world with a pricing model that is both attractive to the small organization and the vendor.
- ❏ Receiving lumps of money is rarely unattractive. But a one–off purchase does not constitute a relationship and relationships are needed to sell deeper into the client. Share of wallet is more important than share of market. The web-services model with its 'continuous payment' structure encourages a more relationship-based approach. Many of us would happily use Office 95, but with web services we would have to use the latest version of Office, whether we wanted to or not.

Impact on IT department

In theory this could be the death of the IT department. Web-services companies would take care of application deployment. The IT department would simply have to ensure that the user-access devices were connected to the web. NB. Web-services lends itself to a thin-client architecture, which would be ironic given the IT department's dislike of PCs.

The IT department would not have to concern itself with:

- Desktop support
- Supporting the servers that were previously used to store/run the applications
- Networking, other than connecting the user–devices to the web.

Thus there would be very little need for a full-blown IT department.

It is most likely that only 'standard' applications will migrate to web services. Office applications and even enterprise applications lend themselves to this delivery model.

A sale and leaseback model may be required to enable the IT department to 'hand-over' the management of its in-house applications.

But this does not stop the IT department deploying its own applications to its users using the web-services model.

Ultimately web-services could yield a transfer of influence from the IT department to the web services provider.

Impact on business

Web-services looks very attractive. It has the potential to:
- Slim down the IT department
- Reduce total cost of ownership of the expensive and fast depreciating hardware. Servers in particular.
- Smooth out cash-flow, what with fewer capital-based purchases
- Provide users with the most up to date software, without the usual expensive rollout costs.

So it looks like a strong contender for the architecture of the future.

But it is not all upside:

- ❑ Can the business trust a third party to manage what is very likely to be confidential data/information?
  - o Storage Service Provision (SSP) goes hand in hand with web services
- ❑ Deploying applications to the user via the network every time a user requires an application will have an impact on bandwidth and hence cost
- ❑ How secure is the link between the provider and the business?
  - o Corporate data will now most likely be shunted across public lines
- ❑ A server-oriented architecture implies risks in respect of single-point of failure
  - o With a PC based model, the users could still get on with some work even if the server fails. With a thin-client based model, a server crash would lead to a 'corporate coma'.

These downsides introduce new risks to businesses that may not outweigh the benefits of the web-services model. One can be sure that the vendors are addressing these concerns.

Outsourcing tomorrow

The future for outsourcing is unclear. It really hinges on whether organizations feel that IT is too core to the business to trust to someone else, or, whether IT is so core to the business they should let experts handle this.

Expect a push from technology vendors towards the outsourcing model. This is the ultimate 'share of wallet' solution. They get the complete (full?) wallet.

The IT industry is still young, but we are already seeing cycles. Outsourcing has been on the ascendancy for a number of years. The number of high profile failures suggested that the market was just about to move back to an insourced model.

But given the new architectures that are vying for oxygen, in particular web services and utility computing, and the fact that their sponsors include IBM and Microsoft, there is a strong chance that it will be a while before outsourcing goes completely out of fashion.

The exception to this will be the organizations that are in themselves large enough to be technology eco-systems, eg. global banks. There is a question mark whether any outsourcing company is big enough to service their requirements. But perhaps there is also a question mark over the future for global megalithic corporations.

Given the trend towards web-based delivery perhaps the next generation of outsourcing should be called cyber sourcing.

Off-shore cyber sourcing

India has proved that off-shore outsourcing can be done reliably and cost effectively. Smart Indian IT professionals recognise their value and increasingly pursue their true value further west. This in turn is pushing the offshore market further east. China and the Philippines come to mind.

India in particular has developed a reputation for supporting and building reliable systems based on the analysis and design provided by the customer. But now India is pushing for the whole software development lifecycle plus the associated project management. In fact India is starting to see technology as something of a detail and is pushing into the BPO arena.

Impact on IT department

It all depends to what extent the IT department relinquishes control. Options include:

- ❑ Complete IT department
- ❑ BPO of a number of business processes
- ❑ Application management
- ❑ Project management
- ❑ Analysis
- ❑ Design
- ❑ Code and testing

The IT department is 'toast' if the first option is chosen (for it). At the other end of the list this would in effect be IT Process Outsourcing (IPO?).

Using offshore services has the effect of distributing the IT function across the planet. Cleverly positioned, one can have a 24x7 functioning IT department whilst paying nobody over-time.

The downside is that IT success is ultimately delivered by good communication. It would seem that phones and email do not compensate for the informal dialogues that take place when people work shoulder to shoulder.

Impact on business

If a job can be done cheaper and to an acceptable standard then "why delay?" is the mindset of business. Even the most ethical and socially conscious have to overlook the 'dignity in labour' ethic if they are to maintain a sustainable business in the 21st century.

Many substantial organizations are already outsourcing complete business processes offshore. The IT department needs to spell out its value to the business if it believes it still has a role to play.

Other developments

Storage

Storage whilst key to IT was always seen as the boring value-free end of technology. This has changed as organizations realise that what they know (ie the data, information and knowledge stored in their IT systems) will determine how fast they can respond to the market. Similarly the nascent broadband society with its video handling capacity will push up the need for storage. Thus storage has started to become sexy.

In relative terms storage is cheap and getting cheaper every day. Even so, the volumes that some organizations are accruing make it expensive. Thus the storage vendors have created solutions that are essentially mapped onto the speed at which the data needs to be accessed. So in general disk space is used for 'real-time' and tape for 'slower-time'. We are starting to see hybrids that provide 'medium-time'.

Bottom line - the faster you want it the more it costs.

NAS

Traditionally online storage technology was bundled into the server / mainframe along with the processor. Increasingly today storage has become decoupled from the processor. This network-attached storage (NAS) can be plugged into the network in much the same manner as a modern printer. NAS technology thus has inbuilt networking and management capability.

Decoupling of processing and storage has enabled the IT department to take a more modular approach to managing its resources.

SAN

An extension of the NAS approach is to segregate storage from the rest of the network. In other words have a network dedicated to storage that is linked to the main (user) network.

The main reason for doing this is speed of access. Fibre optic technology, known for its high data throughput capacity, is a cost effective option because there are relatively few devices attached to the storage area network (SAN). Fibre per se is not expensive, but the device connectors that link the 'storage boxes' to the fibre are. It is this limitation that stops fibre being used in traditional local area networks.

Fibre is inherently fast as it uses light (photonics, see chapter 11) to transmit data. Traditional metal based cabling (twisted pair / coaxial cable) uses electrons (electronics). Light being much faster than electrons gives fibre a natural speed advantage over traditional cabling.

Again, it is too expensive for local area networks that might have hundreds of PCs, server and printers attached. But is perfectly suited to SANs where the number of devices connected is much lower.

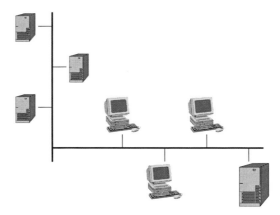

7.4 SAN attached to LAN

Autonomic computing

Autonomic computing essentially describes computers that can look after themselves. The term autonomic stems from our own autonomic nervous system, which regulates our bodily functions, such as heart rate and temperature management without our conscious involvement.

So autonomic computing refers to self-managing computers that require little or no human support. From a staffing perspective this could well be the death of roles such as operator and system administrator. Ultimately this could dissolve all opportunities associated with IT support.

Businesses are looking to squeeze better value from their IT investment. There is a big focus on TCO – Total Cost of Ownership. Autonomic computing looks set to play a large part in reducing TCO, and so will look very very attractive to organizations with large IT infrastructures.

All the hardware vendors are looking at autonomic computing to varying degrees, with IBM seeming to play a lead role. Surprisingly Microsoft is also interested, given its relatively small focus on hardware. Perhaps it is looking to develop the first autonomic games-console?! Most likely it is looking to weave autonomic computing into its Windows operating system. This will then extend this concept into the desktop, thus providing PC support staff with a lot of free time (to pursue other careers).

IBM has created a number of rules that define an autonomic computing system. These include the ability to reconfigure itself to reflect current usage and to constantly monitor itself for optimal usage. More sinisterly it must be self-healing and able to defend itself against threats. Combine that capability with the likelihood that in the future all homes will run off a network on which all your appliances are attached and it starts to look scary.

If your PC suspects you are going to replace it with a younger model, it could well keep you locked out of your home or interfere with the cooling element of your fridge thus impacting on the quality of your nourishment. Check out the film 2001 A Space Odyssey if you want to see autonomic computing at work. Interestingly the computer involved was called HAL, which is IBM if you move each letter along one letter of the alphabet.

Server with a plaster or bandage around it

7.5 Autonomic computing

Where next?

Given the myriad of options available to IT Directors it is difficult to anticipate the new realities. The 'drains up' nature of implementing the options above may make many end-user organizations migrate to some form of outsourcing. How the service companies provide the service is their problem.

'No change' is likely to be the most popular option whilst IT spend remains capped.

Utility computing is an aspiration and so is some way off. Web services has some way to go before all the 'jig saw' pieces are available. I think the smart money will be on thin-client computing in the medium term. But rational logic will always lose out to determined marketing.

In Summary

The architectural options going forward look compelling. Grid computing and utility computing will appeal to the Board, as they are a conceptually easy (but technically complex) 'save money' pitch.

Web services could eventually become the neural system that underpins e-business.

But if outsourcing becomes the way forward then very few people will care about the underlying architecture.

The dilemma is whether IT is so important to your organization that you must keep it in house or whether IT is so important to your organization that you should let motivated experts take care of it.

Test Yourself

29. Grid computing:

    a. Requires the purchase of higher specification PCs

    b. Requires each user to develop system administration skills

    c. Will help organizations squeeze better value from their IT assets

    d. Has its roots in academe.

30. Utility computing:

    a. Is a term coined because a row of servers can make the IT department look like a launderette

    b. Is a term coined to give customers the impression that IT resources can be treated much like water and electricity

    c. Could prove a useful internal approach for IT departments

    d. Requires IBM hardware

31. Web services:
    a. Are always free
    b. Require the user to own an Apple iMac
    c. Are underpinned by Microsoft's dotnet architecture
    d. Is synonymous with application service provision.

32. Autonomic computing:
    a. Can cause servers to be a little aggressive
    b. Will provide operators with a lot more free time
    c. Enables servers to become self-healing
    d. Will contribute to reduced TCO.

33. Outsourcing:
    a. Is almost certainly the way forward for large users of technology
    b. The UK is developing quite a reputation for offshore outsourcing
    c. Outsourcers are very unlikely to adopt grid or utility computing models
    d. A natural extension of IT outsourcing is BPO.

Section 4

Within the IT Department
What happens 'over the fence'

This section examines the structure of an IT department along with how systems are built.

Chapter 8

The IT Department

Why read this? Whilst IT is not confined to the IT department, it does emanate from there. Thus understanding the structure of an IT department will provide you with insight into the way IT works.

The overarching structure

IT departments come in all shapes and sizes. Some global organizations have their IT departments replicated across the planet. Perhaps arranged to ensure that 24 x 7 coverage is achieved without paying anybody overtime.

Some global organizations are endeavouring to bring their IT under one roof, though this throws up security issues, if all the key IT assets are in the one place.

Whether an organization is large or small it still needs to make applications available to the users. In this respect all IT departments are fundamentally the same. The extent to which this is completely handled in-house varies from company to company. Outsourcing, and even off-shoring IT services to third party organizations are on the ascendancy and certainly will continue for the foreseeable future.

The model shown in diagram 8.1 is representative of all IT departments.

The IT Department

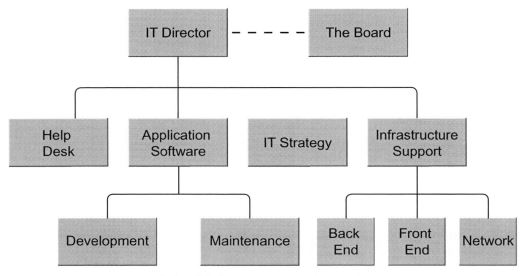

8.1 – IT department schematic

Keep in mind that SMEs (Small and Medium Sized Enterprises) are most likely to outsource their IT as they do not enjoy blue chip economies of scale.

The increasing use of the web as the mechanism for delivering applications will serve to detach the IT department from the users. Whether the IT department is upstairs or in another hemisphere will be academic. This mental-shift will suit both outsourcers and offshorers.

Outsourcing and cyber sourcing will also have appeal to the blue chip organizations, who are quite likely to farm out their 'commodity' applications to a third party. Applications and their associated infrastructure are most likely to be kept in-house when:

❑ They provide competitive advantage

❑ Are too complex/badly designed to be handed over to a third party.

Functionally the IT department will not change. However it is likely that the composition of the IT department in terms of its blend of in-house and third party services will change in the next few years.

CIO / IT Director

The term Chief Information Officer (CIO) has its roots in the US. It fits in nicely with the CxO role standard, where x can equal E, F, P and so on. Some say that it stands for 'Career Is Over', which perhaps reflects that CIOs are destined to not reach the Boardroom unless they get the requisite skills. That is a subject in itself.

In the UK and countries influenced by the UK, the term Information Technology (IT) Director is used. This fits in with the yD model of naming senior roles, where y can equal M, F, HR and so on.

The term ICT (Information and Communication Technologies) is being bandied about. It has lurked within the public sector, particular in education for some time. I don't think it adds any value above the term IT. However it does seem to have stormed the school gates and is in danger of entering the corporate world. Discourage it at every opportunity.

We will focus on the office of the CIO. Typically this is one person but does not need to be.

The office of the CIO can be thought of as:

- ❑   The interface between the Board and its technology investment
- ❑   Being responsible for providing IT related services to the business.

I once attended a presentation given to CIOs where the speaker from research firm Gartner asked for any delegate who reported into the Chief Finance Officer to make themselves known. A few people tentatively put up their hand. The presenter then took the opportunity to give them some unsolicited career advice, by suggesting they change companies.

He was quite right. If the CIO is reporting into the Finance Office then IT will be seen as a cost rather than an investment, and so the CIO will constantly feel downward pressure on her budget. More worrying is that it indicates the Board does not understand the new rules for being a 21st century operation, ie. be IT centric or wither. Again this is another subject.

Smart companies will have their CIO on the Board. Very smart companies will have the CIO sitting next to the CEO on the side of the CEO's writing hand! This is a crude but useful rule of thumb for those considering long-term equity investments. (NB. Health warning. Shares can go down as well as plummet. You are advised to seek advice from your...etc etc)

Help Desk

There is no way of putting this delicately. The help desk exists to protect the IT department from abusive phone calls. People tend not to be at their best when they contact the help desk.

Years ago there were no help desks. The call went straight to a techie (an accepted and inoffensive term for a technical professional) in the IT department. Traditionally social skills and in particular empathy were not seen as a key competency for technical staff. So you can imagine the dialogues when the user phones up to say that their coffee cup holder (more commonly known as a CD drive) is not working.

This would test anyone's temper, particularly if it was interrupting a more important activity. Subsequently help desks were set up with people who were skilled at diffusing tension, and whilst not necessarily technically gifted/trained, could handle the typically trivial problems that made up circa 80 per cent plus of the calls.

Unfortunately some help desks today are not really help desks. You eventually get to an operator and cathartically unload your problem on them. They listen carefully and then offer to get someone to call you back. When you eventually get the call the caller asks you to restate the problem, leaving you wondering what value the earlier person was adding to the service.

8.2 A passionate user

Lines of support

People talk about lines of support. In a nutshell:

- 1st line support – The person who first endeavours to help you with your problem
- 2nd line support – The person, typically a techie from within the IT department, who endeavours to resolve the problem if it can't be handled by the first line person
- 3rd line support – Can be defined by the fact that there is no 4th line support (though sometimes the term is used). If they can't fix it, it can't be fixed. They only deal with problems that 2nd line support can't handle.

Think car breakdown:

- 1st line support – The engineer who meets you at your car. NB. Not the person who took your call and asked you where you broke down
- 2nd line support – The garage the engineer towed you to because they could not fix the problem
- 3rd line support – The component maker who is the only source of knowledge in respect of the broken component.

Applications

Applications provide the real business value. This is the stuff that enables the users to do their jobs more productively. Though this definition might require email to be reclassified.

Consequently this part of the IT department is the most important. Clearly applications need hardware, operating systems and so on, so one shouldn't denigrate the part they play. But it is important to realize that everything is a support function to the 'stars of the show', the applications.

Examples include:

- MS Office
- Client management system

- Air traffic control system
- Trading system.

Games are also applications, but are generally not seen as productivity tools in the work environment. Exceptions to this occur in the military with 'war games' simulators. Having said that the equivalent scenario planning / predictive games are becoming popular in civilian boardrooms.

Applications can vary in terms of size based on:

- Their complexity
- Number of users
- Other variables.

It is not uncommon to have applications that are developed and supported by only one person in a large organization.

At the other extreme I have worked on projects with a team size of 500 people. Thus the applications wing of the IT department can be quite high in respect of headcount.

Structurally each project will:

- Certainly have a project manager (who may also be the developer in a one man team)
- Possibly team leaders
- Definitely one or more developers.

So the staff hierarchy can be quite deep in this corner of the IT department.

Development

Applications need to be written. IT departments have options, which include:

- Write them in-house
- Commission a software house to write them from scratch
- Buying a 'shrink wrapped' 'plug and go ' package
- Buying a hybrid package that whilst requiring some configuration provides the key functionality required.

As mentioned there is a tendency to move away from tailored software, as it is expensive and by its nature unproven, thus constituting a risk.

Whether the IT department writes the software, buys a package or commissions a third party, someone somewhere has to develop, ie write, the software.

In a good market, circa 20% of IT budget is spent on application development. In a bad market it can drop to zero.

Development, like support, tends to be project oriented, in that such activities have a start and a finish date along with other constraints. Development requires taking an idea or concept and actually creating something that performs a business function.

Well-run projects are underpinned by a well thought out project plan.

Support

Support in general can be thought of as the activity that takes place once the item to be supported is in the hands of the users. Examples of supported items include cars, houses, servers and application software.

When an application is first deployed, support tends to be focused on fixing problems, ie debugging the software. As time goes on, the system becomes stable and the users typically request further enhancements. Enhancements can be considered as development, but differ in that they have to be made within the constraints of the existing system. Enhancing software is generally felt to be the next best thing to development in terms of job satisfaction.

There is a tendency for the 'best and the brightest' to gravitate towards development. Starting with a clean canvas can give developers a feeling of being Michelangelo, about to create a great opus that will be their legacy when they go onto meet their maker. I was cured of this illusion when my team leader insisted I wore normal clothes to work, rather than ermine lined robes.

But a key point is that the best developers become the best because they have had experience of support. Average developers write their software with no regard for those that may have to support it years from now. Smart developers recognize that they could find themselves supporting their own software and so take appropriate care. Even if some developers could not care less for the problems they were storing up for future support staff, the prospect that these developers might end up having to support their own software can be quite focusing.

Again the bulk of IT spend is in the support side of IT. Thus making it a more recession proof role than development.

Infrastructure

This wing of the IT department exists to provide the platform or framework within which the applications will run. In this respect it is crucial. The quality of the infrastructure will not only determine whether the applications will be available to the users, but that they are available in a timely and reliable manner.

Thus a well-run infrastructure wing is focused on preventative maintenance and performance tuning, rather than responding to problems.

Infrastructure has both a development and a support element to it. Though unlike applications there is a well-established tradition of buying off the shelf components, eg PCs, routers, and so whilst these have to be configured, in relative terms they have a development period of approximately zero compared to applications. Consequently infrastructure has a support emphasis.

User-access device

Today it is typically a desktop PC and/or a laptop. Increasingly it will also include palmtops and eventually it could well embrace 'head-up displays' onto the car windscreen.

Today desktop support can be subdivided into:

- ❑ PC Support – Responsible for the associated hardware, operating system, printing and networking
- ❑ Desktop support – Responsible for the applications available to the user including email and standard office applications.

8.3 User device of the future

Server

The servers hold shared resources, such as email, databases, files, access to the web and so keeping these available to the users (via their user access devices of course) is critical to the business.

Again preventative maintenance, including capacity planning is the preferred approach. User access rights and networking issues tend to overlap with the servers.

Like PCs, servers are becoming commodity items and are thus quite reliable at the hardware level. The choice of operating system will determine:

❑ The degree of support required

❑ The expertise of the administrator required to provide it.

Network

Broadly speaking networking can be divided into local and wide. Local area networks (LANs) have user access devices attached, whereas Wide Area Networks (WANs) do not. Instead they have LANs attached, typically separated by large distances.

IT departments outsource the WANs to third party suppliers such as the telecom providers. Thus the IT department's exposure to WANs is restricted to the interface between the company LANs and the third party WAN. Network engineers will handle problems at this interface.

The IT department will tend to take charge of its LANs. PC support staff handle PC connections and the system administrators will handle server connections to the LAN.

One of the emerging themes is integrating voice and data traffic onto the one network. The advantage being reduced phone bills. Network engineers will need to extend their skills to embrace telecoms.

Strategy

The pace of change is such that strategy could well become a word to be grouped with water mill and Spinning Jenny. In the past, businesses would plan for the next 5 to 10 years. Apparently the Japanese plan over a century ahead. The problem with such planning is that it does not take into account the perturbations caused by the real world, such as economic downturns, increasing regulation, and globalisation. Those that persist in sticking to the strategy regardless of the environmental conditions are in denial.

That said, businesses need to have a sense of direction, even if that direction changes each month. Traditionally the business strategy is produced periodically and if well communicated will give rise to concerted action throughout the organization.

IT being key to business needs to absorb the business strategy and retune the IT strategy in accordance. If the business strategy is to focus on making the organization more productive then the IT department would focus its attention on the back office and supply chain technologies.

So an IT department that wants to be aligned with the business will have specialists who understand both business and the associated impact of IT. Once the IT strategy is tuned to the business, it will be propagated throughout the IT department.

If the business wants to focus on improved productivity and wants to leverage the web as a channel to market and suppliers, then this will have a bearing on the technologies used. Overnight the new IT strategy could mandate that all projects must use Java as the preferred development language. Thus the business strategy could have a shockwave effect on the IT staff.

This is the challenge for those responsible for IT strategy.

I hope that very soon, rather than the IT department responding to the business strategy, it takes a proactive role and guides business strategy by showing how IT can be used to improve the bottom line. This requires the IT department to have a truly business-focused outlook.

Challenges

It must be said that IT is not like marketing. If the business strategy changes, marketing may have to reword the flyers, or repost a few web pages. Again the impact on the IT department can be severe.

Regardless of changes in business strategy, the business often 'throws curve balls' at IT in the form of:

- New products
- Acquisitions
- New regulations.

It would be uplifting to think of the IT department rushing to the fore and crying 'follow me'. The reality is that they are working so hard to keep up with the business, that the less dialogue they have with the business the less chance the business will have to ask for something new. And herein lies the problem.

Sentiment towards the IT department

The users hold very few IT departments in high esteem. However in my experience, particularly with large organizations, there are pockets of users, perhaps associated with a given project, that perceive IT's support as almost heroic. These are few and far between.

It is practically fashionable for business people to complain about the IT department. Consequently most IT departments have become so inured to this sentiment that they make no effort to defend themselves.

8.4 Business as usual

The underlying cause in my opinion is that IT is becoming crucial to the business, and the business leaders feel insecure because their success is now so entwined with the capabilities of the IT department. The smart leaders recognise that they need to be able to influence IT matters if they are going to succeed.

In this era of high profile scandals, leaders need to pay particular attention to corporate governance, which is very much underpinned by corporate IT governance. Thus poor IT leadership will be a dereliction of duty.

Similarly the IT department needs to improve its PR and go out to the business and explain why things are as they are and what the business can do to get the best value from the IT department. They also need to move the responsibility for an IT system's success from the IT department to the business sponsor.

Such soft skills as PR, influencing, cajoling and negotiating were not seen as key attributes 20 years ago. Those in IT that have them or can develop them are much more likely to have a future in the commercial world.

HR departments need to take note of the 21st century profile for new entrant IT staff. Otherwise the IT department and business will remain unaligned and thus the organization will at best fail to reap the full value of its IT investment. And at worst it will become a competitor's lunch.

In summary

- ❑ The IT department is structured around the provision of applications. Everything else is a detail.
- ❑ The majority of IT spend is in support activities
- ❑ Organizations will increasingly look to IT to help them respond to changes in the marketplace
- ❑ The IT department is seen by many as an ivory tower that is well protected from the business realities
- ❑ The IT department needs to work more closely with the business and to influence it
- ❑ The business needs to understand how new technologies will be key to its success.

Test yourself?

34. Applications:
    - a. Deliver business value
    - b. Are always purchased from a third party
    - c. Always arrive in a shrink wrapped box
    - d. Can be made available via the web.

35. Development
    - a. Is regarded by many IT staff as tedious
    - b. Is only required for in-house applications
    - c. Has it roots in Renaissance art
    - d. Is typically project-oriented.

36. Infrastructure
    - a. Is required for applications to run
    - b. Does not embrace hand-held devices
    - c. In multi-site organizations needs to embrace WANs and LANs

  d. Spend typically reduces to zero in an economic downturn.

37. IT staff

  a. Tend to be Machiavellian by nature

  b. Spend hours by the phone hoping that someone from the business will get in touch

  c. Need to become business influencers

  d. Miss the good old days before help desks.

38. Business staff

  a. Were not designed to work properly with computers

  b. Do not have the sartorial elegance of their IT colleagues

  c. Need to embrace IT for business benefit

  d. Regard operating system functionality as the perfect dinner party topic of conversation.

Chapter 9

How IT Systems are Built

Why read this? To understand how IT systems are built is to understand how one can influence the process in order to ensure the end result is fit for purpose.

Overview

Today IT system development is a labour intensive activity. The IT industry has not yet reached a level whereby the user types in her requirements and the system is produced. This is the ultimate goal and has been for 30 or so years.

Even though there are some CASE (Computer Aided Software Engineering) tools that have automated the process of programming, no one has managed to create a fully automated 'user requirements through to deployed system' tool, which would make application developers redundant.

The IT industry is still young, and as such its practices look relatively immature. The automotive industry assembles cars and the construction industry assembles buildings. The IT industry is not quite at the assembly stage and so system development feels more like creation than assembly.

The problem with creation is that it takes longer, costs more and is prone to introducing problems into the system, unlike the tried and tested components used in assembly.

In fairness the hardware side of the IT industry is mature. The attention to automation and assembly is impressive. Thus electronic engineering deserves its title.

The rigour of the hardware industry stems from the high cost of modifying hardware. There is a tendency to get it right first time, achieving this through formal processes.

Software on the other hand is easy to change. Admittedly the cost of change grows exponentially the later changes need to be made within the project, but this doesn't seem to deter the software industry from generally taking a very casual approach to engineering. Thus the term software engineering is more an aspiration than a description for many software developers.

Certain types of systems require great formality in the build process. These can be classified into:

- Mission critical - There is a lot at stake, eg. Martian probe management system
- Life critical - People could die, eg. Clinical testing system
- Business critical – Money could be lost, eg. Trading system
- Death critical – People could live, eg. Atomic weapon deployment system.

Broadly speaking much greater care is taken in these situations, and the related development projects certainly earn the right to say that they engineer their software.

The real value in IT systems is in the software and not in the hardware. The latter is just a commodity. It's the software that turns a tin/silicon box into an air traffic control system.

Consequently people understand that software should cost a lot. However the software industry could do a lot more to bring that cost down and improve the quality. But the software industry in general doesn't have a great incentive to do this, particularly if poor engineering techniques give rise to greater revenues.

The role of hardware

Hardware is fundamental to IT. Remember the role of software is to make the hardware do things. So without hardware not only will software not run, but there would be no point in running it.

Originally the distinction between hardware and software was blurred. The first computers were primarily hardware with the associated program effectively built into the hardware. Today this is known as firmware and is an appropriate approach for certain types of system, as we shall see.

This approach was expensive and limited the use of the computer, so over the years the software industry evolved. In the process the hardware industry reverted to building standard components, which when loaded with software would turn them into valuable tools.

And so it is today. When it comes to system development, standard components are used. Why reinvent the PC as a user access device when the cost of these devices is so relatively cheap?

There are exceptions to this. If you own a modern car, try looking under the bonnet for the car management system (WARNING: Wait for the car engine to cool down first!). For the more adventurous, the next time you get into a lift, wait until everyone is out and then climb up on to the roof of the cabin. As the lift climbs and descends, look out for the lift management system.

In both these scenarios you are unlikely to find a PC. Car management and lift management systems do not require constant human input and so there is no need for a keyboard or a monitor. In the case of the lift management system the user interface is built into the lift. Again a PC would be overkill for the purposes of selecting a floor.

Both these scenarios represent non-office conditions. The car management system will be subject to great heat and the lift management system will be subject to great electrical interference from the lift power cables. Thus they both need to be ruggedised for their working environments. For both, a PC would be inappropriate. It is more likely that the IT systems involved would look nothing more spectacular than a circuit board sprinkled with memory and processing chips covered with some form of protective material.

Even the supermarket checkouts or cash point machines would be less effective if they adopted a PC interface. In all these cases the hardware has to be tailored for the working environment.

Whilst there are plenty of examples of the need to customise hardware, wherever possible 'off the shelf' hardware is used, because it is cheaper and more readily available.

Thus system development today more often than not is software development, as the hardware elements are purchased 'off the shelf'.

The role of software

As mentioned in the majority of cases the production of an IT system is an exercise in software production. We explored the role of software development tools in Chapter 5.

At this stage it is important to note that software development involves more than simply churning out lines of code (aka instructions). There is a set of steps involved. These steps are based on common sense, though their adherence is not common.

We will look at different approaches to software development, but they all essentially go through the same steps, namely:

- ❑ Feasibility
  - o Whether it should be built
- ❑ Analysis
  - o What exactly should be built
- ❑ Design
  - o How should it be built
- ❑ Construction
  - o Build it
- ❑ Delivery
  - o Accept it
- ❑ Maintenance
  - o Fix it and enhance it.

This is common sense, and is generally applied to building a house, producing a car, or even cooking dinner on a Saturday night.

The typical perception of software development involves banks of programmers, rattling keyboards, listening to music via their headsets. Periods of silence are punctuated with cursing and expressions of elation. This largely describes the Construction phase of a project. Those IT departments/software houses that pay little/no attention to the other phases of the lifecycle are more likely to build not only a system that is not 'fit for purpose', but one that simply doesn't work.

This 6-step model is called the Software Development Lifecycle and sometimes the Waterfall model (See diagram 9.1). The latter title implies that like water, the software development activity cascades down the diagram, Feasibility to analysis, analysis to design and so on. That's how the textbooks present it. Unfortunately life is not like that, and the need to revisit earlier steps is always required.

This fundamental fact has resulted in the waterfall model being dismissed as an approach to developing commercial software. This viewpoint is warranted. The approach was developed for strategic systems that were being built over a number of years. Twenty years ago this wasn't an issue as businesses worked off slower economic clocks. Today economic cycles in some sectors are monthly. The waterfall model, sometimes referred to as the 'big bang' approach, is seen as unresponsive to the vagaries of the real-time world.

Nonetheless all professional software engineers follow these steps. We will see below how this approach has evolved to reflect the new speed of business.

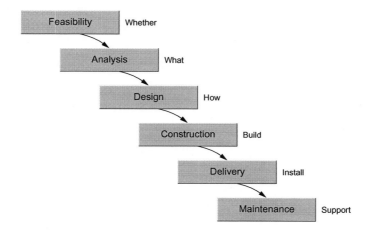

9.1 The Traditional Waterfall Model

The traditional development lifecycle

The term traditional suggests that it was the original approach to software engineering. Again this is true. Whilst it isn't suitable for all projects it does reflect the steps taken by more modern techniques.

Today it still works well where the user is adamant about their requirements and the intended purpose of the system is unlikely to be impacted by external factors.

Let us look at each stage:

Feasibility

As the title suggests, in this stage we contemplate whether the system should be developed. This is driven by questions such as:

- ❑ Can we afford it?
- ❑ Do we really need it?
- ❑ Is it technically possible?
- ❑ Do we have the expertise?

These questions could yield a 'no go' answer. The system development project is thus over.

Also these questions could highlight the need to use a third party, or at least bring in external expertise.

The bigger the risks / opportunities associated with a given project the more likely there will be a feasibility stage.

Many projects do not have a feasibility stage. The need for the system is a 'no brainer' so why delay.

Analysis

The project is now underway. It makes sense to establish what we are going to build before we start building it.

The key word is 'what'. There is a tendency to get struck into the 'how' and even the 'build'. Skip over or under cook analysis and the chance of project failure or at least a 'very sick' project is virtually guaranteed.

So what is analysis? It is simply asking the users what they want and documenting their requirements so that:

- The users can confirm that their needs are understood
- The project team has a frame of reference for building the system.

This is a business-oriented stage. Technology discussions are to be avoided unless there are constraints on the system such as it must use Oracle being the company standard, or it must link to the trading system of the newly acquired investment bank.

Design

Now that we understand what is to be built, it is time to consider how it will be built, ie how the chosen technologies will fit together.

Design can be considered the most creative stage of system development. Though surprisingly there are very few polo necks worn or geometric shaped eyewear in sight. Unlike design in other sectors, system design does not have an address in 'Funkytown'.

An elegant design is, as always, a joy to behold. From a functional perspective it will:

- Meet the users' needs
- Be extensible
  - Easy to extend the system if the users require additional functionality
- Avoid 'vendor lock-in'
  - Does not commit to a technology that will put the IT department at the mercy of the technology vendor.

Good design pays for itself many times over. Unfortunately creativity requires thought, and business managers feel more comfortable seeing staff 'do' rather than think. Consequently design often gets overlooked or regarded as a documentation exercise.

Specifically the designer, more commonly known as the technical architect, will make such heavy hitting decisions as:

- What hardware is to be used
- What operating systems is to be used
- What application development tools and technologies are to be used

If they get this wrong, the system may simply not work, or at least not work in a timely manner.

A key point to note is that no programming takes place at this stage. The key activity is the creative process and the documentation of the associated technical decisions. This technical specification, if well written, will guide the programmers towards writing the right software.

Construction

This is where the programming takes place. Programmers, typically today called developers, will take the technical specification and translate it into software using the prescribed application development tools. Examples include:

- C++
- C#
- Visual Basic
- Oracle
- SQL Server

Some people suggest that there should be an explicit testing stage, prior to delivery. These people have never written software. Testing should be interwoven into the construction process. It isn't smart to save all the testing until the car is built. The Japanese were the first to recognise this.

Component or module testing leads to subsystem testing, which in turn leads to system testing.

For important projects, the testing should be documented. This includes both the test plan and the test report. A boring element of software development, but a critical one, particularly in respect of:

- ❑ Maintenance
- ❑ Legal action.

Good analysis and design would totally deskill the role of programming. The fact that most programmers are well above average intelligence should tell us that there is something intrinsically flawed in the way software is developed commercially.

Delivery

A time of potentially great anxiety. The project team are ready to give it to the users, but the users want to make sure that the system does the job before it is deployed across the organization.

This tension is handled through the process of UAT (user acceptance testing). The criticality of the system will determine the formality of these tests.

If the user representative(s) is happy, the system will be 'rolled out', ie. loaded onto the appropriate operational computers. Hopefully the users will receive training to enable them to get the best value from the new system.

If the system is unacceptable to the user representative the IT department will have to resolve the outstanding problems.

NB. This stage is very important, but becomes paramount if a third party is expecting payment for the delivered system.

Maintenance

The system is now live. Users are using it. It is impossible to test for all scenarios during UAT, so it is likely that more problems will arise in the early stages. Where systems are very complex, some problems may not manifest themselves until years later. This is food for thought particularly when travelling by air.

As the 'bugs' are ironed-out, the system becomes stable. Over time the users may require enhancements to the system as their needs change. It is not uncommon for systems that had an intended in-service life of a few years, to remain operational for several decades. Such systems can often cause new entrant IT graduates to revisit their career plan.

It is important to point out that maintenance is not just an application software phenomenon. The underlying operating system and hardware will also need tuning and enhancements.

It is also worth mentioning that not all projects have such explicit formality between stages. There are many projects undertaken in business that have one or two team members that undertake all stages of the lifecycle. This can make the process appear blurred.

Other approaches

We have majored on the traditional development lifecycle. As mentioned there are competing approaches, which are essentially underpinned by this model. We will take a brief look at what else is available.

Rapid Application Development

As the rate of business change has accelerated a more appropriate approach is required; one that enables the users to be actively involved throughout the development process.

Prior to the nineties, it wasn't possible to build user-friendly IT systems, much less build prototypes as a means to get user feedback. The arrival of the PC spawned the advent of application development tools that made it possible to build 'screen shots' very quickly, thus letting the users provide early comments on what they were going to receive.

These prototypes enabled users to feel part of the development process. Prior to that they gave their requirements during analysis and then had to pray that the delivered system would be the one they had in mind.

Simple user-irritating issues such as background colour or field layout could be resolved prior to delivery, making UAT less of a shock.

Prototyping is not a new phenomenon. In the last decade it has formed the core of Rapid Application Development (RAD), a philosophy that is focused on meeting the users' needs in a timely manner. In a world of tactical IT deployment, if the system is delivered 3 months too late, the business opportunity is missed.

A RAD project is characterised by:

- Users being part of the team
- An evolving prototype, based on feedback provided by the users on a regular basis
- Little documentation
- Accelerated analysis and design phases

In many cases the prototype eventually becomes the operational system.

The RAD approach is most suitable when:

- The user is not clear on their requirements
- The system is required in a relatively short period of time (weeks/months as opposed to years)
- The system does not have a high degree of complex processing
- The system is not in any way mission, life etc. critical.

Taking a flyer on the analysis, design and documentation would be a foolish approach to developing critical software. Many systems are required, that whilst important, are not critical. Typically these are back office administrative systems.

But please note RAD has a part to play in critical systems in respect of the user interface. The behind the scenes processing can be handled using the traditional approach.

RAD is not a new concept, but is growing as more organizations start to use 'visual' development technologies and see the value of involving the users at every stage.

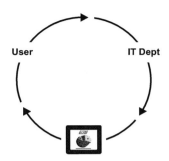

9.2 Continuous prototyping

Incremental delivery

Often used by software houses, which are working on large IT systems. It helps the cash flow if there is a series of deliveries rather than one big bang. This makes staged payments more palatable to the customer as they are actually getting usable functionality in exchange for money.

Traditional development might hang interim payments off the completion of the analysis and design phases, but these are abstract deliverables in the eyes of most clients.

For both software houses and IT departments this approach has the benefit of enabling the project team to test/fine tune the development environment at an earlier stage than with big bang. To discover that there were problems with the development tools in a traditional project would leave little time for resolution.

Also this model embraces some of the RAD principles in that early delivery of subsystem A will elicit early user feedback, which can be woven into subsystem B and C.

High risk

High risk can relate to any phase of the project. Perhaps the users are unclear or not in agreement in respect of their requirements, or a non standard piece of kit is to be used, and no one on the development team is certain that it will work within the overall design.

Usually these risks are coupled with high stakes systems, eg. development of a multi-national fighter aircraft.

The high-risk approach takes the traditional model and produces a prototype at every stage of the waterfall. During analysis this prototype would be to confirm user requirements. During design this would be to test for example, performance or connectivity.

The prototypes result in feedback that flows back into the development process. As the project progresses certain risks will be eliminated, whilst other unexpected problems will emerge. Imagine developing an IT system with the lights out to imagine what this must feel like.

Clearly the additional risk assessment through prototyping at each stage will extend the development phase and the cost. Where the high-risk approach is used, the significance of additional costs is far outweighed by the consequences of success/failure.

Software development philosophies

When it comes to building systems there are in fact two choices to be made, one in respect of lifecycle and one in respect of software development approach. The former we have covered, the latter is a philosophical one, which we will now explore.

All IT systems can be looked at in terms of their:

- Processing
  - What the systems does
- Data
  - What the system does it to.

The two philosophies we are about to look at embrace both of these, but their emphasis on each is different. Without further ado:

Structured

The first attempts at software engineering were based on the structured approach. The focus was on the processing, ie what the system is to do. So if a staff management system was to be built, the focus would be on what it should do.

A process of functional decomposition would take place (See diagram 9.3 for a retail banking example). The system could be fragmented into subsystems, for example talent acquisition, staff development and appraisal management. Each subsystem would be fragmented further, for example development might be broken down into director, management and staff.

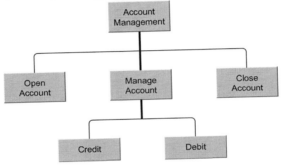

9.3 Process oriented design

This would provide a very clear view of what the system was to achieve. Having done that consideration would be given to the associated data requirements.

This approach was very much in line with logical system thinking. It reached a peak in the seventies. Methodologies such as Jackson. Yourdon and SSADM originate from the structured school of software development.

Having had thirty years to evaluate this approach, there is plenty of evidence to support its strengths and weaknesses. Its main strength being that it captures the system logic, which is essential to developing sophisticated systems.

Its weakness is that it does not handle changing requirements very well. What started out as a cleanly designed system, now from a software maintenance perspective looks like a 'botch job'. The reality is that data requirements change very little over time, whereas the processing requirements do. If one was to develop an IT system for a Phoenician retail banker, you would find that their data requirements are much the same as today's banking systems. The approach to processing would be quite different.

In fairness to the structured approach it was created in an era where systems did not need to change very much over time. IT systems were strategic tools and so unlikely to change on a regular basis. The structured approach has trouble in handling ever-changing requirements.

There are many examples of 'structured' IT systems in use today. This reflects the power of the structured approach to building 'industrial strength' software. However their maintenance is generally a painful activity.

Object oriented

The new kid on the block is object orientation (OO). Even though it is new, it is circa forty years old. The arrival of the Java language in the last decade has brought it more into the mainstream.

Whereas structured is process oriented, OO is data oriented. Building the system around the data, as any Phoenician banker will tell you, is the way to develop systems resilient to changing processing requirements.

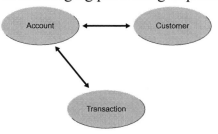

9.4 Data oriented design

Taking our staff management system above, the OO approach would be to focus on the data objects, for example, employee, training course, pool car, pension and so on. Having identified the objects (strictly speaking data classes, read an OO book for more details), one can than consider what one does to staff. In most businesses this would at least include hire, fire and promote.

Focusing in on the data objects allows the user and IT staff to have meaningful conversations about real word things. Structured data types were limited to dates, numbers, characters or Booleans (True/False). OO allows the programmer to define data types such as bus, hamster, employee or whatever is appropriate to the system being built. This is much more intuitive for the user.

In theory OO promotes:

- ❑ Reusability
  - o Reusing software reduces costs, saves time and improves reliability
- ❑ Extensibility
  - o Modern systems need to change in line with the changing business environment
- ❑ Maintainability
  - o If software is easier to maintain it will have a reduced total cost of ownership.

I say 'in theory' because even though most people buy into the OO philosophy, they do not necessarily practice it. Reusability in particular is very patchy. Very few organizations have their own library of reusable objects. There is still much 'wheel reinvention'. We are getting there, but it is taking a long time.

OO requires an altruistic attitude. If I am building a system, it is easier for me to write the software with just my system in mind. Focusing on reuse will increase my design effort, which will eat into my budget and calendar. And all this to make subsequent users of my reusable objects look good. If OO is to take off then senior IT management need to incentivise staff to take an altruistic approach.

OO is the future. It marks the IT industry's transition to maturity. Reuse, or standardisation, is the mark of a mature industry.

But what of its weaknesses? OO does require greater management of the software development process. If an object is too system specific, it will not be reusable. If it is too generic it will be of no use to anyone. Getting the balance is the challenge.

Going forward

A hybrid of Structured and OO is the best way forward.

Some people regard the OO v Structured argument to be passé. The move towards enterprise applications where the software modules embrace specific functions within organizational departments, for example payroll and recruitment seems to have smothered the debate. The talk now is of component-based development (CBD). Whether each component is developed using OO, Structured, neither or both is felt to be academic to the user.

I would counter that it does matter to the user as poor software development ultimately costs the user more. Component-based software can enable poorly written software to be presented with a polished veneer.

Software engineering as a topic has been 'off the agenda' for some time. Smart business leaders will start to ask the IT department to what extent they are adopting an OO approach. Not because the board has 'discovered' software engineering , but because they want to ensure they are getting best value from their investment.

In summary

- Building systems today is more often than not a matter of building software
- Hardware can and does get customised but this is avoided if at all possible
- When developing software one has to consider the lifecycle and the software development philosophy
- The choice of lifecycle is dependent on a number of factors including risk, the user's ability to articulate their needs and the urgency of the delivery.
- The choice of philosophy will be determined by the extent to which an organization is keen to reduce its development and maintenance costs over time.

Test yourself?

39. Design
    a. Requires a certain minimalist dress sense
    b. The best software designers have an Apple iMac at home
    c. Done well, it can reduce the amount of testing required
    d. Requires thought.

40. Hardware
    a. Being more malleable than software is easier to modify
    b. Is a key element of an IT system
    c. In some cases is tailored to the application
    d. Is often bought 'off the shelf' for use in IT systems.

41. RAD:
    a. Requires users to be told what they need at regular stages throughout the project
    b. Embraces the use of prototypes
    c. Has a keen following in the atomic energy management sector
    d. Requires extensive documentation.

42. OO:
    a. Is data oriented
    b. Is reflective of practices used in mature industries
    c. Could never be used along with the Structured approach
    d. Is a hot topic at Board level.

43. Delivery
    a. Is a great opportunity for users and IT staff to 'hook up'
    b. Can be stressful, especially where third party software houses are concerned
    c. Should include user training
    d. Is the end of the project. The team can now disband.

Section 5

New Technologies
What's hot today and what will be hot tomorrow

The Internet, World Wide Wait (sorry Web) and e-business are covered here, along with what to expect in the foreseeable.

- ❑ Chapter 10 –What's hot today
- ❑ Chapter 11 –What's hot tomorrow

Chapter 10

What's Hot Today

Why read this? This chapter explains the drivers that caused the technology market to veer out of control, the aftermath and the associated buzzwords. Understanding how we got to today will help you reduce the chance of repeating the mistakes made by others.

New technologies defined

New technologies are those that organizations are harnessing to gain competitive advantage (in a good market) or drive out costs (in a bad market).

In the last five or so years the focus has been on web based technologies. Without doubt the web is the planned medium for practically all emerging technologies. Even the more traditional technology vendors such as Microsoft, Oracle and SAP are building their vision around the web.

Some will argue that Wap, 3G, Wi-Fi and interactive television (more on these later) are exceptions to this definition. However I believe their creators have developed these with the intention of at some point embracing the web.

It would be silly not to, given that the web provides a global, free and technology androgynous (vendor independent, in English) communication/transaction solution.

So for the purposes of this section we will focus on web-based technologies.

The dotcom era

This was a period that reached full frenzy in the late 1990s and cooled rapidly from March 2001. It had a number of notable characteristics:

- ❑ Making a profit was no longer seen as the primary aim for a corporation
    - ○ It was secondary to 'buying' new customers
- ❑ Venture capitalists could not unload their capital fast enough
- ❑ Due diligence extended to whether an idea was 'cool' or not
- ❑ Dotcom start-ups regarded 'burn rate' (ie the rate that they consumed cash) as their critical performance indicator
    - ○ There was a direct correlation between burn rate and coolness
- ❑ The perceived value of hi-tech companies meant that over 50% of companies (by market capitalisation) on the world's major exchanges had cash reserves of 6 months or less
- ❑ Being over 30 and not being a paper billionaire was a constant source of social embarrassment.
    - ○ For me anyway.

13.1 Dotcom board meeting

Silly valuations

The new dotcom economics enabled start-up companies to be valued at many millions even though they hadn't turned a profit and had no intention of doing so. That would be a problem for a future owner (read 'sucker').

The frenzy enabled the dotcompanies to achieve these stratospheric valuations through simply floating a low percentage of the stock, typically 5%. A high share price would be inevitable as investors rushed to get a piece of dotcom action. This allowed the dotcompanies to regard themselves as having a value of, in this case, twenty times the value of the issued shares.

This is much the same as saying that it is reasonable to assume that a 100m sprinter can maintain their pace for 2,000m. Try it if you are not convinced.

The scarcity of buyable dotcom stock caused a 'get rich quick' public to buy without any regard to the underlying fundamentals of the stock.

Everyone was infected

Traditional technology companies such as Microsoft, LogicaCMG, IBM et al saw their share price 'head north' for no other reason that they were technology players. If your day job was to boost the share price then this was all fine and dandy.

Even though the dotcom boom took the non-tech companies by surprise, they wasted no time in creating their own Internet divisions, with a view to partially spinning them off and thereby boosting their growing but relatively languid share price.

No greater fool

The stock market in a bullish climate is underpinned by the Greater Fool Theory. An individual buys the stock at an unrealistically high price on the basis that there is a greater fool who will buy it from him at an even higher price.

Come March 2001 the market had run out of greater fools. The market analysts who had become drunk on the 'new economics' were starting to sober up. At that point the dotcom companies were deemed as 'bad news' and the race was on to sell. Their share price went into freefall and the dotcom billionaires club was replaced by the 90% club.

The entry condition was that your share price had to drop more than 90% of its initial public offering (IPO) price. It was a far from exclusive club.

This rocked the world stock markets, given their dotcom weightings. It also sent respectable and profitable technology companies into a downward spiral. Up until recently the markets have punished the Technology Sector. Many of us working in this arena have witnessed what can only be described as a 'technology nuclear winter'.

Nothing learned

Unfortunately it is not the first time that this has happened. The history of the markets is littered with stories, including the South Sea Bubble (1720), Tulipmania (1637) and more recently the creation of the railroad industry in the US. All were characterised by unnatural exuberance, followed by market collapse. If the dotcom era follows what has become known as the Gartner 'Hype Curve', the market will pick up but the growth will be modest.

We know for certain that we have passed the exuberance phase. The question is how far down the market collapse phase are we and how soon will the modest upturn commence?

There is still one last chance to become a dotcom gazillionaire if you know for certain when that upturn is about to commence.

There are indicators that the markets have started to forgive the Technology Sector. However only time will tell whether this is the start of the upturn or just what some call a 'dead cat bounce'.

Key technology terms

The dotcom hysteria caused people, particularly those in marketing, to speak in foreign tongues. Words and phrases like disintermediation, 'clicks and mortar' and 'click ass' came out of nowhere. Many such terms have been consigned to the history books.

However some of the buzz-terms have survived and have since been joined by post-dotcom additions. This section will take a look at the important terms:

e

This raises a fundamental question, what does 'e' stand for? When most people refer to e they think of the web. But it is important to remember that e means electronic and electronic embraces more than the web.

Specifically e relates to:

- ❏ Any aspect of IT, from legacy systems through to modern technologies
- ❏ Leased lines – Hired communication links that are both very private and very expensive
- ❏ Dial-up – The ability to use one's telephone line to gain access to a computer elsewhere.
- ❏ Virtual Private Network (VPN) – A network that has better security than the Internet, but is less costly than leased lines.

Not all of the above embrace the Internet, but all are e-based.

The point is that e-commerce, for example, does not necessarily have to mean web-commerce. But keep in mind that the end-game for all the vendors is for e to become synonymous with the web.

e-commerce

The dotcom era focused on e-commerce. The ability to sell via the web was seen as a very cost effective channel through which to reach the market.

One of the weaknesses of the dotcom era was that in their haste to relieve customers of their money via the web, the vendors had failed to consider how they might fulfil using this medium, or even use their traditional IT systems. The lack of integration between customer-facing technologies and back-end fulfilment technologies was destined to cause problems.

This is one of the key areas of focus for many companies today.

e-business

Originally e-business was a noun that referred to an organization that used the web as its only route to market. Today it is used more as a verb. Whilst one can conduct e-commerce, ie sell, it is also possible to market, recruit, buy, pay etc. etc via the web.

Thus e-business can be thought of as a term that refers to conducting some or all aspects of business electronically. So e-commerce is just one aspect of e-business. And so those that are focused on e-commerce are still trapped in a dotcom mindset as the wider opportunities lie in e-business.

Internet

The Internet is in essence a network of networks. It emerged from work carried out by the US Department of Defense (DoD) Advanced Research Projects Agency (Darpa). The Agency recognised that the network linking the US DoD's military establishments was vulnerable to failure if any of the installations on the network were destroyed.

Thus they created a technology that would enable the remaining installations to continue to communicate if one or more 'nodes' of the network became 'unavailable.

TCP/IP

The technology in question was a piece of software called TCP/IP. It can be thought of as a dynamic route planning service. It thus enables networks to take a more flexible approach to transferring data. Prior to TCP/IP, networks acted like dumb commuters. Despite knowing that the local station is closed, the commuter makes no effort to plan an alternative route to work. Some might say this is far from dumb.

TCP/IP being more like a smart commuter routes communications between the source and the destination based on what intervening computers are available on the network. The commuter in this case adjusts her route in line with the options available.

Thus TCP/IP provided a high degree of fault tolerance in the DoD's military network.

Beyond the DoD

Other big networks around the globe adopted this impressive technology to increase their own reliability. Eventually the main networks across the planet including that of the DoD were plumbed together to form what we today call the Internet.

Thus the Internet can be thought of as a network of networks that communicate using TCP/IP.

WWW

The World Wide Web, or for many, the World Wide Wait, can be thought of as an application that runs on the Internet. In much the same way that email is an application.

It can be thought of as a giant library of information. This information is delivered to the users via web pages, which are stored/built on web servers, many of which are owned by Internet Service Providers (ISPs).

What makes the WWW so interesting is the fact that:

❑ The information can be delivered in a 'rich' format. Not just text, but sound, pictures and video

❑ Web pages can be made interactive, thus enabling them to capture and deliver information

    o This in turn lends the WWW into enabling users to conduct transactions

        ▪ These transactions can be of a financial nature

        ▪ Thus making the WWW a potential medium for e-business.

There are issues in using the Web for financial transactions and we will look at this very soon. Nonetheless the beauty of the Web is that it is more or less free and provides all organizations with a 'ready to use' infrastructure for doing business globally.

We are only beginning to see the potential that the Web has to offer.

Portal

A portal can be thought of as a gateway into the Web. In theory every web site in the world is a portal. However true portals have certain distinguishing characteristics:

- ❏ They provide information to the visitor
- ❏ They are used as a brand reinforcement tool
  - o Building trust online is more difficult than in the physical world. Thus many companies position their web sites as portals
- ❏ They often provide links beyond their own site to other related sites on the Web.

Internet plumbing

The most high profile sites are typically associated with:

- ❏ Search engines
  - o Google, Overture
- ❏ Directories
  - o Yahoo!
- ❏ ISPs
  - o MSN

These companies provide services that are interwoven into the fabric of the web and so they get heavy usage, which increases their profile, which increases their usage and so on.

Online businesses

Some vendors have achieved portal status, Amazon and eBay being two examples. It would appear that the most successful trading portals are those that are focused. Typically when people know what they want, they go to specialists rather than general-purpose websites.

Amazon is testing this theory by expanding its own offerings beyond books. Possibly the lesson is to:

- Get well known through having a laser beam focus on a particular service
- Once well known, exploit the brand by diversifying into other services.

It is too early to say whether this approach will work. The number of successful online businesses is currently very limited; never mind the number of such businesses that are looking to leverage their brand.

Stickiness is key

One of the dotcom hangover words is stickiness, which is a reference to the:

- Length of time visitors stay at your site
- Frequency with which they return.

Dynamic content is a key element to a portal's success. Search engines, directories and news related web sites have natural stickiness. The key objective for those that have invested in a portal is to cultivate this characteristic.

In theory a portal with high volumes of focused visitors offers the perfect opportunity to:

- Sell advertising to other organizations who share an interest in the visitor community
- Cross-sell services to buyers within the visitor community

To a large extent this theory has yet to be proved and many organizations have spent millions in the vain hope that the theory is correct. Again time will tell.

e-Government

Governments across the planet are at varying stages of providing their citizens with better services at reduced cost. The general approach to achieving this is through citizen-friendly portals.

With a monopoly over its customer base, the main challenge for the Public Sector is ensuring that all citizens have access to these portals.

The race to e-Government will ensure that portals remain in the spot light for at least the next 5 years.

Intranet

An intranet is a private network that utilises Internet technologies, ie:

- ❑ TCP/IP – for underlying communication
- ❑ Web technology – for sharing internal information.

The ideal scenario for any business is to have just one intranet. Anything over one creates communication barriers.

Intranets are a key element in an organization's knowledge management approach. At the very least they provide the ability to communicate by email. Smart organizations are using intranets to capture wisdom and make it available to those that need it, when and where they need it.

Extranet

An extranet, sounds like a spare intranet, but isn't. An extranet is an intranet that allows controlled access from the outside world. Thus companies can:

- ❑ Allow suppliers access to, for example, their stock management systems
- ❑ Allow customers access to, for example, their market research database.

The key point here is that the access is controlled. Through some form of secure login, the external visitors will have access to a limited number of services on the intranet.

Access control applies both to intranets and extranets. Allowing staff free access to the salary server could work out quite expensive.

Java

Java is one of those truly techie words that has escaped into the business arena.

Firstly, Java is a programming language, and like all other programming languages it exists to build applications, which is the software that helps businesses do business. So Java has a direct impact on business (like any other programming language). Java has some interesting characteristics:

- ❑ It is platform independent
  - o The motto is "Write once, run anywhere'. The key business benefit here is that it protects the IT department from being 'locked' into a single 'platform' vendor, eg. IBM, as many languages are designed for just one platform. Once an organization invests heavily in writing software in a platform specific language such as RPG/400, it in effect gets locked into the underlying platform, in this case the AS/400, and thus places itself at the mercy of the platform provider. Java protects the IT department from such scenarios

- ❑ It is bandwidth friendly
  - o Unlike traditional languages, which encourage large amorphous applications, Java's applet approach enables programmers to build applications made up of smaller components. This has great advantages when the application is delivered to the user via a network, given the constipational impact of large applications. The Java model is kinder on the network, as it enables the user to download only what is needed. Invoking a Java written word processor results in the download of just the basic editing suit. If at some future point the user requires a spell checker, the associated applet is downloaded. This is important to IT Directors because bandwidth, the volume of data a communication link can take in any given time, is one of

   the most expensive technology resources managed by the IT department

- Microsoft dislikes it
    - This is not in itself a benefit, but it does offer an alternative to Microsoft's 'very platform dependent' tools. Microsoft's particular dislike is that it allows its developed community to migrate away from the Windows platform. Many competitors to Microsoft are in support of Java for its industry balancing effect. But history shows that when Microsoft decides it doesn't like something it is just a matter of time before it ceases to be relevant. Watch out for Microsoft's C Sharp (C#) alternative.

Java's bandwidth friendliness has made it the programming language of choice for web-based applications. It forms part of a larger suite of technologies known as J2EE (Java Version 2 Enterprise Edition), which aims to provide the full architectural framework for IT systems going forward. Interestingly a single vendor, Sun Microsystems, controls this vendor independent framework.

As you might imagine Microsoft does not share this vision, and so has its own dotnet architecture drip-feeding into the marketplace. In fact the main title fight in the technology arena is the 'battle of the architectures'. IBM and even Oracle see themselves as contenders as well. But the fight to watch is J2EE versus Microsoft's dotnet.

Exchanges

Exchanges have been around for centuries. They physically allowed buyers and sellers to meet and transact. Negotiation techniques included:

- Bartering
- Auctions
- Reverse auctions
- Sealed bids
- Take it or leave it.
    - Very popular in today's supermarkets

The dotcom era threw up the notion that this approach to trading could be replicated electronically via online exchanges. The dream was that business supply chains would move away from inflexible partnerships to a more dynamic real-time and frictionless (no people involved) model. Exchanges would exist at each junction in the supply chain, where buying and selling systems would thrash out the deals.

13.2 "I've spotted a buyer!"

This model is very likely to dominate at some point, but not for another year or two at least. In fairness the investment banking market has being doing this for years. If you want to see how wrong it can get cast your mind back to Black Monday October 19th 1987, when the Dow Jones Industrial Average plunged 500 points despite the fact that the economy was good and there was no negative news in circulation. That's what can happen when you leave trading to the computers.

The last couple of years have almost seen the demise of practically all the public exchanges, ie those where buyers and sellers could just 'walk in' and trade. So the public exchange marketplace is non-existent today. Again public exchanges have a future. They just don't have a present.

The main causes for public exchange failure appear to be:

❑ Lack of liquidity in terms of either buyers and/or sellers

    o Plenty of buyers, but few sellers doesn't work. Or vice versa

❑ Some buyers lost the plot in respect of balancing price and value. First generation exchanges became a place to beat up the sellers on price.

Private exchanges, whereby the buyers and sellers are pre-registered to trade appear to be on the ascendancy. The one buyer-many sellers approach is growing in popularity with big companies that want to leverage their relationships with their suppliers and have a single point of access for procurement.

Exchanges are a natural extension to e-business. Unfortunately the first generation suppliers were a little too ahead of their time.

13.3 "Sorry, no jeans or t-shirts"

Firewall

A key component in ensuring that your intranet/extranet is protected from the outside world is the firewall. This can be thought of as an e-bouncer. A firewall like a nightclub doorman does let people in, but only those that meet the criteria.

Similarly the doorman will under certain circumstances influence who can leave the nightclub.

Think of firewalls as controlling the flow of data both into and out of the network. Thus companies want to ensure that:

- ❑ Only certain external people, if any, have access to the network
    - o Data flowing out
- ❑ None, some or all internal people have access to the outside world
    - o Data flowing in
    - o Many companies these days take a dim view of those that spend their 'working hours' surfing the net.

Hardware or software?

It is possible to buy software that acts as a firewall. Though the more security conscious an organization is the more likely that the firewall will be hardware. The security paranoia stack is as follows:

1. Off the shelf software

2. Off the shelf hardware

3. Tailored hardware – nothing unusual about the development process

4. Tailored hardware - where none of the developers understand the full workings of the firewall

5. Tailored hardware – where the development team go missing on delivery.

Guess which is the most expensive? Funnily enough an even more secure solution that is cheaper than all of the above is what is known as an 'air gap'. In other words there is no connection between the internal network and the outside world. Unfortunately the impressive security benefits this yields are more than offset by the isolation that not being connected to the web brings.

Capabilities

The more you pay the more it can do. Firewalls can for example:

- ❑ Double up as virus checkers
- ❑ Detect unsuitable content
  - o This is extending beyond simple word searches to contextual analysis
    - ▪ Technology can now read emails and act on their contents
- ❑ Detect correspondence between employees and recruitment companies and redirect it to HR
  - o Triggering HR into succession planning mode

- Log who has visited where on the Internet
- Force external users to log-in prior to entering the network
- Keep a copy of retrieved web pages to speed up the delivery should someone within the organization subsequently request these pages.

Firewalls are the technology equivalent of a very vigilant security guard.

Broadband

Broadband relates to bandwidth. To recap bandwidth is a measure of data throughput. So a bandwidth of 56kps suggests that 56 kilobits of data per second can be pumped through the 'pipe' (aka channel). The connecting medium may be wire, fibre or wireless (or a combination of these).

The term bandwidth has its roots in telecoms, more specifically voice comms or telephony. Voice is not bandwidth intensive. In this respect it is very similar to sending emails. Thus voice and 'text' traffic are often referred to as narrowband.

In the last decade advances in networking electronics and photonics (think fibre optics) have enabled users to send images and even video (a succession of images) across a network. Broadband can be considered as video quality bandwidth. Anything above 0.5 megabits per second (circa ten times the speed of traditional dial-up modems) can be thought of as broadband.

Broadband was a hot topic during the dotcom era because television and the web were on a collision course, and only broadband could make that a reality. Broadband remains a heated topic today as wireless phone vendors struggle to deliver true broadband (ie. 3G) to the palm.

Ironically despite the lack of broadband to the doorstep/palmtop there is a surplus available across the planet. One of the 'get rich quick' schemes in the telecoms sector was to lay as much fibre optic cable as possible on the basis that someone would buy the company prior to them having to deliver any services. The anticipated frenzied build up to provide broadband services would alleviate them from having to build an actual business.

But unfortunately two events upset their plans:

- ❑ The end of the dotcom era
- ❑ Physicists invented a technique to get almost infinite bandwidth from just a thin piece of fibre.

Both these events caused a collapse in the price per megabit. Thus the planet is threaded with thousands of miles of unused (aka dark) fibre. Roll-forward a couple of thousand years and imagine how vexing this will be for archaeologists.

Payback might be guaranteed if the telcos can convince us to part with large sums to pay for services such as perhaps holographic conferencing. It may well happen, but don't hold your breath.

XML

This harmless and in the main unexciting TLA (Three Letter Acronym) is already playing a key part in making frictionless business a reality. Its significance is such that it warrants being described with the other buzz terms in this section.

What is it?

XML (eXtensible Markup Language) is a language that is used to define data structures. It can be thought of as a form definition language. By form, I mean for example a driving licence application form. Today this form is paper based and is usually processed by a human, which is both time consuming and error prone. With XML one can create an identical electronic form, which can be processed by a computer. XML provides a mechanism for defining the form fields, eg. <Full name>, <telephone number>, <age>.

What is more, XML places no restrictions on the type of fields invented. That's the extensible part! So there is no reason why the form cannot be extended to include <favourite car colour> and <zodiac sign>. Such flexibility makes XML the perfect starting point to create one's own language. In this case it could be called DLML – Driving Licence Markup Language.

What's the fuss?

There are a number of reasons:

Openness – XML is not under the control of a single vendor. It was created by the World Wide Web Consortium (W3C), which is made up of industry players, but is not controlled by any of them. Thus XML is less likely to seduce us into becoming part of somebody's revenue agenda.

Interoperability – There are many incompatible systems in existence that lie along various business flow chains. XML can be used as a way of standardising the flow of data between these systems. Thus there will be no need to go out and buy single-vendor enterprise wide applications. ERP and CRM players take note.

Such interoperability will make it much easier for companies using disparate technologies to work together. So expect a flurry of joint ventures over the next few years.

Flexibility – XML allows you to define whatever language you like. Be it ECML - Ecclesiastical Crocheting Markup Language or RAML – Real Ale Markup Language, XML will enable like-minded folk to get talking electronically without the need to overhaul their IT systems.

Comparativity – By using XML on the Web, it will be possible to label the data held on web pages such that it is visible to XML reading software (aka software agents or bots). Thus if a user wants to get the best price on a Ford Cougar, they can simply send their bot off to gather all the web pages that contain the price of such a car. Having been spared the need to:

- ❑ Trawl the showrooms physically
- ❑ Trawl the web manually

Such XML agents can more or less instantaneously get the best price.

XML is likely to force vendors into a commodity situation. Prices will be much the same wherever you go, ie low, causing vendors to compete in other areas such as quality of service, after sales care etc.

What's the future for XML?

The future looks bright. In one fell swoop we have a vendor independent data structuring language, which addresses the needs of the e-world, both web and elsewhere. It could put a big dent in the revenues generated by the systems integrators and the enterprise application developers. It is sufficiently flexible to cope with existing display technologies, such as PC, TV and PDA. And also for forthcoming display technologies such as 'head up' display glasses and virtual reality.

However where it will really make an impression is in comparative shopping on the web. If you sell commodity products/services make sure your site is XMLed (more specifically xHTMLed), otherwise your business will be invisible to comparative shoppers.

More terms can be found on our website at www.auridian.com/gloss.

The Issues

Bandwidth

It is many people's understanding that WWW stands for the World Wide Wait. For those of us who have a telephone dial up connection, waiting for web pages to download is often an exercise in self-control. This is not helped by the Jean Michel-Jarre egocentric Flash animations that sit between us and what we need from the site in question.

The issue here is bandwidth, which is the volume of data that can pass along a channel or pipe in a given time. In this particular example it is most likely passing down a twisted pair copper cable laid by your telecoms supplier.

A telephone dial-up connection will comfortably download graphically-light web pages. And thus one could argue that web site builders should ease off the fancy graphics and animation.

But the issue relates to a bigger picture. In the UK, Broadband Britain is an aspiration for the Government. This ambition is mirrored by most other industrialised nations.

Originally cities were built along waterways. Latterly road and rail have become the main arteries on which to plan new towns. What concerns

Government is that the information superhighway will soon be a determining factor for where:

- ❑ Towns are built
- ❑ People chose to live
- ❑ Businesses choose to locate
- ❑ Tourists choose to visit.

Thus if your town, city and/or country is not wired up for the 21st century you are in real danger of becoming an economic backwater. So bandwidth is not so much an issue for today, but one for tomorrow.

With a better infrastructure in place, ie broadband into every home, it would allow office bound workers to work from home and so:

- ❑ Improve the quality of their lives
- ❑ Reduce the accommodation bills of the employer.

Everybody wins.

Even more acute is the problem of not having any access at all. This growing gap between those with access to the WWW and those that do not has been termed the digital divide.

If this is not addressed then all plans for e-government will be on hold, or worse still it will create a new social division between the information 'haves' and 'have nots'.

Security

Security is both a perceived and real threat to the uptake of new technologies. The belief that using one's credit card on the web will lead to fraudulent usage of the card is both a remote but real possibility.

Why is it that some people are happy to put their credit card behind the bar or allow waiters to take their card out of their sight when paying for meals in restaurants? Both these activities are more likely to result in card fraud.

But to a large extent that is academic. Perception is everything and many people do not want to conduct financial transactions on the web because it doesn't appear to be safe.

Security also embraces privacy and trust. The thought that our health records could be tampered with by mischievous kids is unnerving. The fact that you had a limb amputated in what you thought was a routine tonsillectomy operation might seem hilarious to some pranksters, but not to you. Unless security is resolved, new technologies will expose us these sorts of scenarios.

In respect of conducting business online, trust is a key element. Can you trust the other party you are dealing with? Over time more business will be conducted where the two parties never physically meet. This is ripe territory for fraud. The modern gangster's weapon of choice will be the keyboard. If the dream of frictionless 'exchange based supply chains' is to become a reality, then security needs to be resolved.

Beyond trust there is the issue of authentication. You believe you are dealing with someone you trust, but how can you be sure? Just because the email has my email address as the sender does not necessarily mean that I sent it. Such malpractice is known as phishing. This needs to be tackled.

Despite the vested interest of big business and banks, security remains an unresolved aspect of web commerce. There are a number of security architectures in existence, the most comprehensive of which is PKI (Public Key Infrastructure). But this has many variations and is seen as too complicated and expensive to implement.

Please note that most reputable online vendors use a variant of PKI. You can tell if PKI is in use by the little padlock icon at the foot of your browser. The problem here is that this variant of PKI allows you the user to be sure that the vendor is who they say they are, but it does not allow the vendor to authenticate you. Thus online merchants sell their wares knowing that they are exposed to fraud. Clearly they have weighed up the risks and are happy to live with this, but it is clearly unsatisfactory.

What you know	Eg. Password
What you have	Eg. Security card
What you are	Eg. Fingerprint

13.4 Levels of security

Security techniques are starting to move from what you know (eg. a password) to what you have (eg. a credit card with embedded security chip) to ultimately what you are (eg. iris, voice, fingerprint recognition). The latter is more commonly known as biometrics. Security is one area where we are guaranteed to see rapid advances in the next few years.

Commercial

Commercial activities need to be underpinned by a legal framework. The web throws up all sorts of issues, including:

- ❑ Whether an email constitutes a contract?
- ❑ What jurisdiction rules over an online shopper in one country buying faulty goods from a vendor in another country?
- ❑ Can one country legislate against offensive content that is held on a server in another country?
- ❑ When does ownership of goods transfer when trading across borders, given that the trade documents are likely to arrive significantly after the actual online transaction has taken place?

In the UK email has contractual significance. In fact in the UK a verbal agreement has contractual significance. The big issue in the case of email is proving that the supposed sender was indeed the real sender. The PKI security infrastructure incorporates the ability to authenticate the sender.

Many jurisdictions do not recognise the contractual nature of electronic communications and therefore traders need to ensure that the lands in which they do business electronically do not leave them commercially exposed.

At a more basic level, definitions and messaging formats need to be agreed for the associated e-paperwork, for example orders, remittances and invoices. This is not a technical problem. The big challenge is getting agreement amongst the trading community.

Interoperability

The dotcom era was focussed on selling via the web. The issue today is integrating this 'channel to market' with the back office fulfilment systems.

The complicated name for the issue of linking computers together is interoperability. Say this without stuttering and you are well on your way to becoming a consultant.

From a vendor's perspective this is known as systems integration (SI) and it represents a big business opportunity. The reason being that linking together two sets of technology that were never designed to work together is a messy, and thus a risky business. This is good news for SIs, whose clients are willing to pay high margins to offload the risk.

Unless your organization was created during the dotcom era (congratulations for still being in business) or beyond, you are very likely to be faced with integrating modern technologies into your existing legacy/pre-funky technology investment.

The Opportunities

One could argue that that one man's issue is another man's opportunity. So technology service organizations that address any of the above issues are addressing well-documented needs.

Thus the following areas look set to grow in the foreseeable future:

Bandwidth

❑ Java/C#
  o These are both bandwidth friendly programming languages.

Security

❑ Authentication
  o Providing a security framework that enables parties to verify who they are dealing with is still 'up for grabs'
❑ Biometrics
  o This is a fast growing authentication approach
❑ Security Policy

    o It is felt that the security opportunity is not so much in technology as in defining and enforcing security policy. The best firewalls in the world will not compensate for users who leave their password on a post-it stuck to their monitor.

Commercial

- ❑ Trade
  - o Particularly the area of e-documentation. Buying for example train carriages from another country involves significant paperwork. Moving this paperwork online will make it easier to conduct such transactions online
- ❑ Web law
  - o Today the WWW is the (World?) 'Wild West'. There are few precedents and so few people know/understand the associated legal issues. The law cannot keep up with advances in technology. This is a great opportunity for the more agile law firms
- ❑ Exchanges
  - o Exchanges do have a future. Today they are mainly private, but over time public exchanges will form a natural part of doing business on the web. One could say that sites like Amazon.com are first generation exchanges. But true exchanges will embrace dynamic pricing and more innovative price agreement techniques.

Interoperability

- ❑ XML
  - o This simple data labelling language will be very much in demand as industries attempt to standardise their data formats. The big thrust initially will be in converting proprietary formats to those that are industry agreed

- EAI
  - o Enterprise Application Integration is a branch of systems integration that focuses on developing 'software adapters' that enable two disparate systems to communicate with each other. It will slowly slip into oblivion if XML really does deliver as promised. And so can be thought of as an interim opportunity
- Middleware
  - o This is the underlying messaging software that enables cross platform communication. There are a number of evolving/mature standards in this area. The 'under the bonnet' nature of middleware makes it something of a mystery to most people. Those that understand middleware are in a strong position to provide the 'corporate glue' needed to bind systems and thus organisations together.

Post dotcom

The dotcom era ended in March 2001. This is the point that the Nasdaq turned into the Cresta run. At this point the market grew hostile to technology companies and thereby technology. Much of this hostility was redirected self-loathing for being so foolish as to think that betting on technology (or anything for that matter) was a sure-fire win.

Traditional technology companies got the same flak as the upstart dotcom boutiques. The Technology Sector entered a nuclear winter.

13.5 The party's over

Organizations that rushed to acquire an e prefix or a .com suffix discretely reverted back to a more traditional naming convention. Some organizations aligned themselves too closely with the Internet, and have now been scarred for life.

E-commerce during the dotcom era was seen as too important for the IT department and so was transferred to the marketing department, albeit temporarily. Thus the IT department which in many cases had little influence in an organization's dotcom dreams yet was seen as the villain of the piece.

The last couple of years have been difficult for many businesses. IT aside the market has been tough. These companies have had to cut costs. Many of these companies, still upset with the IT department's behaviour (!), failed to see that IT was the key element in their cost management programme. I personally have witnessed companies cutting the costs on their cost-cutting IT projects. This has been referred to as trying to lose weight by 'cutting into the muscle'.

Smart end user organizations recognise that technology is key to helping them bring their costs into line with revenues. Those that have already achieved that are focusing on using IT to differentiate themselves from the competition.

Smart companies recognise that IT is more than just the stuff the IT department does. They have come to terms with their dependence on IT and are looking to exploit new technologies to gain competitive advantage.

In summary

- ❑ The dotcom era was a period of madness whereby profitability was no longer viewed as an indicator of business health
- ❑ E-commerce was superseded by e-business
- ❑ XML will be a key element of e-business going forward
- ❑ Security, bandwidth and commercial/legal issues need to be resolved before e-business can truly happen
- ❑ Post dotcom, IT continues to be crucial to business survivability
- ❑ Web business has a long way to go before it becomes mainstream. IT will play a key role in helping organizations to drive out costs.

Removing the outstanding obstacles will be a source of opportunity for entrepreneurial organizations.

Test yourself?

44. The dotcom era:

    a. Was the final nail in the coffin for IT

    b. Was more focused on sales than delivery

    c. Made it socially embarrassing to not be a paper billionaire

    d. Was underpinned by the fact that technology companies could do no wrong.

45. e:

    a. Implies Internet only

    b. Embraces all forms of electronic activity

    c. Is a recreational drug that can only be purchased via the web

    d. Was coined as a term to show how we had moved on from d-commerce.

46. A firewall:

    a. Is purely a software based technology

    b. Should be located by the main entrance to your home or office for maximum effect

    c. Exists to stop unauthorised access to a private network

    d. Exists to control unauthorised web surfing.

47. Issues impacting the uptake of web business include:

    a. The lack of an agreed industry-wide security framework

    b. The inability to download products such as stereo systems or cars directly to the buyer at the time of purchase

    c. The lack of standards relating to documentation such as invoicing

    d. The problem of trying to pay for goods by putting coins into the PC's CD drive.

48. Post dotom:

   a. There is still a need for new technologies
   b. Many organizations need to integrate their funky websites with their mundane internal systems
   c. Getting rich quick through technology is a lot harder
   d. Anyone with a memory span greater than a goldfish will be more cautious about any forthcoming technology market upturn.

Chapter 11

What's Hot Tomorrow

Why read this? This chapter provides some insight into the way in which new technologies could be deployed over the next few years. Thus there is a strong element of futurology in this chapter.

Introduction

Imagine the technological progress made in the last forty years being compressed into just a few years and you will get a feel for the likely rate of change ahead. The possibilities will only be limited by our imagination.

Interactive Television

Overview

One could argue that everyone has interactive television in that it is possible to change channels as it suits the viewer. Over and above this many cable and satellite viewers can:

- Watch football matches from different angles
- Send emails
- Order pizza

The interactive element is improving at a relatively fast rate.

So where next for i–TV?

Convergence

This is a very popular word in technology circles. Most typically it relates to the convergence of telecoms and IT. i-TV looks set to be the intersection of the convergence of IT, telecoms and broadcast media. In this respect the potential for i-TV is almost infinite.

Welcome to the carpettop

We have had desktops, laptops and palmtops. The television is showing all the characteristics of becoming the fourth 'top'. To some extent this started when the first personal PCs were nothing more than a box with a built in keyboard (eg. Commodore64). They needed a television to run, though admittedly its role was one of dumb monitor. However this spawned the concept of carpettop computing. Perhaps we could go back even further into the seventies. Little did those TV paddle tennis players realize that they were the original carpettop pioneers.

Convergence again

Broadcast media can be broken down into content and infrastructure.

The content traditionally relates to films, documentaries, cartoons and so on. The infrastructure relates to the mechanism by which the content is delivered to the living room and displayed there.

Increasingly content embraces anything that entertains or engages the user (to use the term viewer implies passivity). So this can include video games, web surfing, television banking and/or word processing. In business terms, if the user will pay for it, it can be called content.

Traditionally television content was delivered in an analogue format. With the migration to digital, the content can be regarded as data. Thus the content can be displayed on any digital content supporting device, eg. PC and palmtop. So the display options for broadband have widened. The delivery of the content can be via cable or wireless. More importantly broadcast media content can utilize telecoms and IT delivery infrastructures. NB. The telecoms and IT infrastructures themselves are converging. Overtime all networks will be able to support, voice, data and broadcast media.

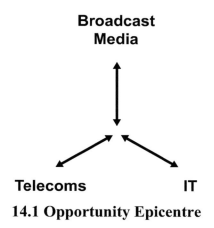

14.1 Opportunity Epicentre

Broadband

For broadcast media, or for that matter any form of graphically rich media, to be delivered in a real-time manner, it will be necessary for the infrastructure to have broadband capacity. Essentially broadband is a term that describes a network that can cope with real-time video. Ubiquitous broadband is some way off, but today cable companies are serving up IT, telephony and broadcast media services on the same medium, thus accelerating the uptake of broadband.

The Box

An interesting question will be whether the television starts to look more like a computer or vice versa. Try this simple experiment. Put your PC in a corner of your living room. Try watching a DVD from your sofa. Next sit right in front of your TV imagining that you are writing a letter. In fact try imagining it whilst sitting on the sofa. As you will see both devices are optimized for their current function. So we may well see a next generation TV that embraces both modes of operation.

So that we do not leave wireless out of the experiment, grab the nearest mobile phone. Imagine watching 'Gone in 60 seconds' or some other high-octane movie on the mobile's screen. Now imagine word processing on the screen. Sadly the makers of 'smartphones' have yet to do that experiment.

The Web

Given that the web is free it makes sense to utilize the Internet as a delivery channel. However we will have to wait until the web has bigger data pipes. But once this and the security bit is resolved (content owners seem to be a little sensitive in this respect) there is no reason why i-TV cannot be served up via the web.

Hypermedia

Most people are familiar with multi-media, ie content that embraces one or more of the following:

- ❑ Colour
- ❑ Graphics
- ❑ Sound
- ❑ Video.

Most people are familiar with hyperlinking, ie the ability to click on a word or graphic on a web page and be transported, across hyperspace apparently, to another page.

Well what happens when you mix hyperlinking with multi-media? Well you get hypermedia, which allows users to click on video objects and be transferred elsewhere. So if you like James Bond's car, just click on it and the order form comes up. What better time to sell to you when you are sitting at home with your 'commercial body armour' off dreaming about being Mr Bond. The TV now becomes a point of sale device in every home. Advertisers will like that.

Content jukeboxes

The problem with programmed television is that you have to watch your favourite programme when it suits the programming company rather than you. Video on demand (VOD) is an emerging concept. Those with cable suppliers have a variant called Near VOD (NVOD). Each film, in what is typically a very limited offering, is set up to run several times per day at intervals that are proportionately related to the film's cinema success. Again the programmer is in the driving seat.

Where we need to get to, and I believe we eventually will, is true online content jukeboxes, whereby the user can chose from all digitally stored content. Had a tough day? Start the evening with some dinosaur documentaries, followed by a Charles Bronson vigilante flic, working your way through your feelings to end on a few episodes of Friends.

Once this becomes available people will be stressed out by the choice. We will then likely see the emergence of ultra-niche lifestyle self-programming. With the likes of Cosmopolitan, GQ and Vanity Fair providing content advice. In fact your evening may well start off by logging onto a lifestyle portal, letting it choose your evenings entertainment on a pay per view basis.

Targeted advertising

The idea of a paid service determining which adverts the user should be exposed to is nothing more than an exercise in consumer segmentation. The attraction for advertisers is very clear. Today's television advertising, by its very nature is untargeted and thus intrusive and so more likely to cause brand damage than sell product.

But highly focused advertising to an 'opted in' audience is a win-win for all concerned.

Take this one step further. In theory there is no reason why the advertiser can't ascertain personal information about the target. So let's imagine the advertiser is a travel agent. If the target is known to be wealthy, or at least lives in a 'wealthy post code' they are exposed to the luxury holiday adverts. Conversely the not so well off are subjected to more affordable options. Thus the promotion is highly tuned not only to the target's interests/aspirations but also to their budget.

In what will be an increasingly challenging market for all, the travel agent's ability to get some margin from many of the poorer targets will be just as valuable as cherry picking the scarcer rich.

There are of course privacy implications. But it might suit some individuals to give trusted organizations permission to distribute their personal details appropriately.

Impact on business

Smart technology companies will endeavour to reposition themselves as close to the IT, Telecoms and Broadcast Media intersection as possible.

TV advertising will grow rapidly as the future model migrates from being push to pull based, with recipients requesting information on particular products and services. This will become more attractive to smaller organizations as they can target their limited advertising spend with laser focus.

The advertisers themselves will work more closely with the content providers, ie the producers of films, documentaries etc. The programmes will in effect become vehicles for the advertising.

The broadcast media players will most likely merge with the web players. With companies choosing to focus on infrastructure or content.

Impact on the IT department

Today much of broadcasting is done on dedicated kit. This is gravitating towards using standard computing components. Thus the IT departments in the Broadcast Media Sector will start to take on more televisual responsibility.

End user IT departments will have the challenge of managing the bandwidth hungry content coming onto their network. This will make content management and storage two big growth areas in the IT Sector.

Impact on consumers

Consumers will be able to enjoy 'designer TV', with adverts that reflect their aspirational needs. They will joke about how broadcasting companies once decided when consumers should watch their content.

It is very likely that the 'soaps' will remain scheduled in order to create the social buzz that underpins their success.

Knowledge Management

Overview

From data to wisdom

First we had data. Phone numbers and birth dates are examples. Data is the oxygen of IT. Computers exist to process data. Though data per se is useless to the user.

However information is useful. This can be thought of as processed data. A stack of CVs has no value, but the answer to 'how many Java programmers live in Paris?' will have to certain people. One might say that computers convert data into information.

What is even more important is making an interpretation of the information. Is 5,000 Java programmers a good enough reason to set up a web services boutique in Paris? The answer to that question involves the processing of information in the context of other relevant facts that usually reside in the head of a subject matter expert(s). One might say that knowledge is information that has been processed by a brain. Thus knowledge can be highly opinionated.

Alternatively knowledge can be thought of as a collection of loosely related information sources that can be linked together to form opinions and so make decisions. At least one of these sources will be a human brain.

14.2 The Value Stack

If we take this to the extreme knowledge acted upon (or in some cases actively not acted upon) is wisdom. Wise people are not only knowledgeable, but they are adept at applying what they know, when appropriate.

Today

Data management and information management are well established. Knowledge Management (KM) has been threatening to make a breakthrough for some time. There are those in the IT industry that believe KM has come and gone, having made very little impression in between.

My own view is that KM is much more than IT and that if an organization does not have a KM strategy it be well on its way to extinction. For service based (read people based) companies this is an imperative.

Intellectual capital

First we had Personnel Management, which acknowledged the human aspects of the workforce. Then came Human Resources, which despite the word 'human' has the feel that people are assets to be stocked and utilised much like paper clips. Latterly we are seeing Human Capital Management, which acknowledges the human side but is pointedly only interested in what the people know and how they apply it. A more euphemistic term is Talent Management. But Staff Brain Clustering services or Wetware Aggregation department would do equally well.

In any case the underlying theme is something called intellectual capital. It doesn't show up on the balance sheet today, but it will do in the next few years. One could say that intellectual capital is the difference between the value of the company (market capitalization) and the value of the non-human assets. If this equates to greater than zero, then your people are adding value to your organization. Less than zero then they are destroying value.

So service companies in particular will become increasingly valued by the intellectual capital they possess. Shareholders in general are either oblivious to this or take it in their stride. Otherwise at the close of play each day, shareholders would sell their holdings as workers left the office, on the off chance that they did not show up for work the next day. Whilst this is an extreme, once intellectual capital becomes more mainstream people related matters will have significant impact on a company's perceived value.

Yes but what is KM in practice?

It is a bit of an airy-fairy term and no two people will give you the same definition. I see KM from two perspectives:

- ❑ Enabling the organization to 'hunt as a pack'
- ❑ Ensuring that the organization only ever makes the same mistake once.

Hunting as a pack means sharing intelligence. Big organizations in particular are often feudal in structure with the emphasis on feud. The sales director of equities will not share what they know about their clients with the people in fixed income. They don't want to lose control of the relationship, even though both parties sharing would be to the benefit of the organization and customer.

Making the same mistake once is a sign of wisdom. But big organizations through lack of communication, repeat projects across the world and fail to learn/share the lessons from their initial experience.

It all boils down to communication. Having one intranet, where everyone can communicate with everyone is a start. Global databases detailing customers, suppliers, market intelligence and so on would be a great help. A global directory of who is good at what would enable the organization to solve its own problems, rather than bringing in expensive consultants (or me).

Why isn't it happening?

KM involves the messy business of people and politics. Asking a sales person to share their customer intelligence is much like asking them to donate their kidneys to their employer. They will need to be very incentivised to do so. Attempts at KM that do not acknowledge this reality are destined to fail.

Traditional hierarchical organizations headed by feudal lords are more often driven by the power struggles at the top than anything market facing. The only cure is a flatter organization where those involved are incentivised to share.

KM needs to be sold to the people before it is deployed.

Impact on business

As mentioned the impact will be disastrous if KM is not sold to the stakeholders. To make it stick the motivational tools available will need to be remodelled.

Once buy-in happens then it's time to 'pull up the drains'. The organization will need to be reengineered to facilitate knowledge sharing.

The organizations that move fastest in this respect will be the most able to adapt to market changes and thereby increase their chances of long term survival.

Look out for terms such as 'real-time organization' and 'adaptive organization'. In many respects these are just new labelling for knowledge management.

Impact on the IT department

The IT department will truly become the centre of the business universe. In essence their role will be to ensure that the data, information and knowledge flow freely throughout the organization.

Failure on the IT side will lead to a corporate coronary.

Impact on consumers

As the internecine turf wars become a thing of the past, corporate energy will be directed towards the customer experience. Customer satisfaction will be a key performance indicator in respect of one's KM investment. Thus KM and brand are proportionally related.

The World Wide Web

Overview

The World Wide Web is not a new technology, but it is an evolving one. As mentioned previously, for many it is the World Wide Wait (just in case you forgot to find it funny then). Searching for information requests the patience of Joab, the sleuthing skills of Sherlock Holmes and the logic skills of George Boole.

So whilst the WWW has changed our lives dramatically, it still has much scope for improvement. Let's take a look at where we will most likely see the greatest improvements.

Speed of retrieval

There are a number of 'choke points' between the information you need and your PC. These include:

- ❑ The server on which the web page resides
- ❑ The network(s) that links the server to your ISP's server
- ❑ Your ISP's server
- ❑ The connection between your IT department's web server and your ISP
- ❑ Your organization's LAN and your PC
- ❑ Your PC.

The information superhighway is well advanced and much of the Internet autobahns are 'fibred up' to handle broadband traffic. The superhighway enables the major ISPs to link to each other and other web based resources.

The idea of an information superavenue, where there is a broadband connection linking the ISP to the user is well underway, but has some distance to go before broadband becomes standard for users. Remember one needs broadband to access video quality information.

The user's PC rarely impacts the speed of retrieval unless it is concurrently undertaking a number of memory intensive tasks and the hard disk is a few bits short of being full.

Server technology is dropping in price dramatically and the concept of blade servers, (see Chapter 2), makes upgrading a simple task. Perhaps even more importantly the ability to cluster servers together to shore up idle capacity (Grid Computing, See Chapter 7) will play a significant role in ensuring that ISPs and web server owners will be better able to respond to variations in demand.

Should the TV industry ever choose the web as the delivery medium, it will need to ensure that the web will be able to cope with the delivery of real-time content. Timing is everything in comedy and so this programme category may be the last to migrate on line.

The WWW of tomorrow will be based on super-fast networks, linked straight through to the user's doorstep. The web servers will cooperate with each other in terms of processing (aka load balancing) to ensure timely delivery of content.

Information retrieval

Today Boolean logic is required for anything other than the simplest of queries. Knowing your ANDs and ORs (inclusive and exclusive) along with the use of broad matching, wild cards and speech marks is essential to accessing the information you seek.

Today's web experience presumes the user's occupation is electronic circuit board design. Trust me on that if it seems an odd comparison.

So there is a lot of scope for improvement. Attention seems to be focused on:

- ❑ The user interface
- ❑ Intelligent searching

In terms of the user interface there is gravitation towards 'natural language'. Websites like askjeeves.com imply that they are handling natural language, but they are not. Try typing in "I haven't the slightest interest in pizza". Apparently Domino's Pizza is targeting customers like you! No reflection on the site, but that is more or less the state of the art today.

True natural language would allow such non-Boolean phrases as:

- "I cud mu'da a pizza"
    - Think high profile Glaswegian homicide detective
- "Gimme a pizza"
- "I yearn for a Pizza"

It would pick up on colloquialisms and deduct that the user is predisposed to pizza and 'time to doorstep' appears to rank high in respect of the user specification.

Taking this one step further, the user would not have to type anything and so the refrain "Oi! Compu'a. Pizza. Now!" having been decrypted by the voice synthesis software would then be translated into a search engine recognizable format and dispatched to a search engine optimised for local services.

Natural language has yet to make a real impact on the user experience, though more modest variations of it, eg. voice activated word processors and mobile phones show that it is not a new concept.

The user experience

Businesses and even governments are keen to service their customers/citizens at the lowest possible cost. The web is a perfect medium in this respect. Over time, unless one is willing to pay for a real human to be involved in the transaction, it is most likely that the main point of contact will be a computer.

Today we can order provisions, books and the like online, so this is well underway.

The big theme will be personalization. Again not a new concept, it is just a question of how far it can be taken.

Online supermarkets can/will have the capability to:

- Replace background muzak with your favourite tracks
- Tailor special offers to your purchasing profile
- Contrive special offers based on items you put in your shopping cart last time, but felt guilty at the last moment and took them out, for example champagne or chocolate

- ❑ Recognise your aspirational profile, based on your purchasing history, and recommend products that are consumed by those that you 'aspire to be'
- ❑ Using your purchasing history, adapt the websites responses accordingly. So regular purchasers of Ferrerro Rocher chocolates would be welcomed with "Thank you for visiting us again. You are truly spoiling us" daubed across the home page.

Wouldn't it be nice if your online banking, for example, were conducted through an interface that looked and sounded like:

- ❑ Jennifer Lopez
- ❑ Brad Pitt
- ❑ Thomas the Tank Engine
- ❑ Marvin the Paranoid Android?

These avatars could really inspire the user to return to the website.

Access devices

Today the WWW is mainly accessed via the PC. Other options today include:

- ❑ TV
- ❑ Kiosk
- ❑ Mobile phone / Palmtop

With the exception of the PC the experience is generally poor. These will improve over time. If mobile phone manufacturers persist in trying to offer us web access devices then they will need to address the display issue. Watching Gladiator through a mobile phone display just isn't the same.

Options to rectify this include:

- ❑ Foldable screens – Get on the train. Unfurl the screen, which could also include a touch sensitive keyboard, onto the table and there you have your very own 2D web access device
- ❑ Head up displays – State of the art fighter pilot technology is used to project the display onto your Georgio Armani 'head-up' occiali. Imagine you are on a train. You put the glasses on. The attractive individual sitting opposite sees news and investment-banking data

feeds streaming down your glasses and presumes you're a business professional. The perfect tool for public transport lechers.

Take the head up displays one step further. Using a technology called 'haptics' (check out the film Minority Report for more details) you can manipulate a 3D holographic 'screen' using hand/arm movements. It will look like a variant of Tai Chi to unknowing observers and will certainly unnerve other passengers.

Shopping

Perusing a holographic shopping mall lined with only the items you are likely to ever need will be the end game. The ability to filter out items that eg. 'may contain nuts' will increase the user experience.

Returning to today, the shopping experience is of variable quality, with Amazon leading the way. But what if you want to get the best deal?

Let's imagine you want to purchase a car, let's say a Ford Probe, and pay as little as possible. Options include:

❑ Visit all the showrooms

❑ Use a search engine and type in "Price of Ford Probe"

The former will take many hours and will involve being sold at. The latter will throw up thousands of pages, many of which will have nothing to do with cars. So again it will be a time consuming task.

What if one could simply go onto the web and access a search engine that limited its searches to data that was labelled using an internationally agreed convention, such that searches would only pull up relevant pages?

That is what XML is about. See Chapter 10. This is the data labelling specification for everything from 'Price of a Big Mac' to 'Printer Warranty Period". Those that sell via the web will be well advised to ensure that their web pages make use of the agreed labels to ensure that they are retrieved when a customer goes comparative shopping.

The good news for merchants is that they will be included in all relevant searches. The bad news is that they will face price pressure in a manner they have never experienced. Comparative online shopping will put the consumer in the driving seat.

Today we have a pseudo variant of this. Certain sites will offer to go and get you the best deal, for example in respect of a hotel room. However the search is limited to the hotels that have already signed up to the web site in question. The XML variant of this, or whatever might replace XML, will allow shoppers to roam freely with no intermediaries taking a slice of the transaction.

The only problem here is not a technical one, but one of getting the merchants to agree on the labelling and data structures (aka metadata).

Impact on business

Even though the dotcom era has come and gone, the Web will become more important than ever as organizations look to reduce the cost of marketing, sales, delivery and payment.

Impact on the IT department

The IT department saw the web taken away from them during the dotcom era and handed over to Marketing. If the business hasn't already asked the IT department to integrate the web to the main IT systems within each department, then it will.

The IT department looks set to move to centre stage. Each department, front end and back end, will be knocking on the IT department's door looking for help in driving down their costs.

Once the costs are under control the IT department will be busy, should it decide to take the initiative, helping the business gain competitive advantage through using web technology.

Impact on consumers

Idle chitchat with the bank clerk will be a thing of the past, as you are moved onto a channel that befits your lifetime value to the bank. Banks are just an example; this will apply to all businesses. Person to person interactions will be confined to niche services and the ultra-rich.

Automated transactions will suit those of us that are generally 'time-starved'. The ability to shop and bank when it suits you more than offsets the opportunity to make new friends whilst queuing. I presume?

By the way I have come up with a post dotcom phrase in the vein of B2B, B2C etc that really captures what will be a rare form of interaction in years to come. I am sure it will become ingrained into the global consciousness once it hits the streets. Pray tell you cry. Face-to-face I reply, or F2F. Original or what?

Nano-technology

Overview

Think small and scary.

Miniaturization is a key driver in the world of technology. The ability to store more data on a hard disk or squeeze more electronics onto a square centimetre of chip is a key element of competitive advantage for hardware vendors.

The world of nano-technology looks set to accelerate us to the end game in terms of miniaturization. The term is based on technology that has dimensions in the order of nanometers.

Nanometers are very very small. In fact one nanometer is one billionth of a metre. The building blocks at this level are individual atoms and molecules. The equivalent of a current-carrying wire need only be one atom thick. Data storage would take place at the subatomic level, with a bit being represented by an electron.

The fundamental working component is the nano-robot, which typically will perform some useful function and reproduce itself a finite number of times.

The challenge is to assemble these nano-robots. Manipulating atoms is no trivial exercise and so electron microscopes are used to monitor the process. Electrical and magnetic fields plus carrier molecules are used to dock atoms together.

These nano-robots need to be programmed in order to become useful and replicate. It is unlikely that Visual Basic or other high level programming languages will be of much use. We will see a reversion to machine code programming (See chapter 5), or even atomic programming.

In parallel to this, the area of genetic programming is evolving. Underpinned by artificial intelligence, nano-robots will not only do what they are programmed to do, but adapt to the environment they are in through 'on the job' learning.

So let's take a look at nano-technology's potential:

Nano-medicine

The medicine tastes a little crunchy, well that's because you have just swallowed a hoard of nano-robots, which will have been programmed to destroy:

- ❑ Cancer tumours
- ❑ Viruses
- ❑ Bacteria.

Millions of these atomic submarines will cruise your veins hunting out the enemy. They will, if necessary, replicate themselves until the job is done.

14.3 Nano-tech workers

Nano-warfare

The converse of medicine is chemical warfare, or in this case nano-warfare. As one can imagine, nano-robots could easily be leaked into the water supplies of a target city. No point killing your future workforce, but making them unconscious for a number of days should give you enough time to take charge of the key installations and supply lines.

In fact should the workforce get that 'uprising feeling', there is no reason why the nano-robots could not be remotely controlled to reawaken from their dormant state in their host's body.

Only the paranoid survive

Nano-technology is like genetically modified food only better, or worse, depending on your perspective.

The production process would need to be carried out in literally perfect conditions. Small variations in temperature or pressure could cause the nano-robots to mutate. Their behaviour might then be unpredictable and worst still uncontrollable.

Be ready for nano-technology.

Impact on business

It's a little too early to say. Possibly we might see the arrival of intravenous CRM (customer relationship management), but it would of course be highly unethical.

Impact on the IT department

Again it is too early to say. Though the property values for housing IT departments will plummet, if one's entire IT infrastructure can fit in a matchbox.

Impact on consumers

Don't be an early adopter.

Photonics

Overview

Photonics is a generic term for technologies that operate at the speed of light. Traditionally the IT industry is based around electronics. In essence this means that electronic devices operate at the speed of electrons (Do a degree in Physics if you need more information, or befriend a physicist, whichever is easiest), which whilst fast, does not hold a candle to photonics.

Let's take a router, which is responsible for directing data traffic from one network to another. If one lifted the lid off an electronic router one would see an array of circuit boards with chips attached. Take the lid off a photonic router and it looks more like the inside of a telescope, all prisms, mirrors and lenses.

Traditionally cabling, most notably twisted pair and coaxial, is based on electronics. Fibre optic is a photonic cabling technology and thus inherently much faster and so can offer higher bandwidth.

Why does it deserve a mention? In much the same way as society has experienced agrarian, industrial and information revolutions, the move from electronics to photonics will herald a quantum leap (literally) in computing.

Thus photonics is funky, sexy and the new new thing. Upstart communications companies have broken away from their electronic daddios to develop next generation photonic devices.

Imagine a single lane track that can flower into an infinite-lane motorway. That's the potential of photonics. White light can be broken down in theory to every possible hue of every colour. Each unique colour represents a lane. The term associated with this is DWDM (Dense Wave Division Multiplexing).

To put it in perspective we already have enough fibre laid across the planet for each of us to be having holographic conferencing with someone on another continent. Once the other photonic components are in place, this will be a reality.

Impact on business

Faster is usually better in terms of technology. But another benefit of photonic components is that they are electronically silent and so do not emit signals that eavesdroppers can tap into. Thus they are inherently secure.

Whilst fibre is not expensive, connecting to fibre is. Each connecting device needs to have what is in effect a laser gun, which squirts data bits onto the fibre. These are expensive and thus using fibre as a local area networking technology is not cost effective. However it is used in wide area networks where there are no devices attached and storage area networks where there are relatively few (storage) devices attached.

Impact on the IT department

Photonics is likely to impact those responsible for managing the networks, particularly in respect of the interbuilding communications. This is most likely to be outsourced to a third party.

Impact on consumers

Consumers will not necessarily see a change, as the quicker responses delivered by photonics may be dulled down by the 'last mile' technology, ie the cabling that runs from the local exchange into the consumer's home. It is very unlikely that the telecom operators (telcos) will dig up the 'last mile of twisted pair cables and replace them with fibre. Why? Because this will be a cost to them, yet they will have to share (at the insistence of the local regulatory body) the new medium with other competing telcos.

Possibly the enhanced bandwidth capabilities delivered by photonic technologies will lead to cost reductions that are passed onto the consumer. This may be wishful thinking as the network providers may be desperate to get payback on their overcapacity. More likely we will be offered new and interesting services that we do not really need.

Wireless

Overview

Infrared

We have wireless today. We have had it for years. Most television owners are reliant on infrared technology to keep movement to a minimum whilst concentrating on the riveting content. Infrared as a communication medium works but is somewhat limited. It requires a 'line of sight' link and doesn't' pass through walls or people who irritatingly position themselves between you and the TV (commissioning the production of a parabolic mirror to suspend from your ceiling is a workaround). Infrared is unlikely to be a key communication technology of the future.

Cellular Radio

Another wireless option is cellular. Think mobile phone. The concept is based on the manner in which the service provider, eg. Vodafone, makes the service available. Each cell defines a geographical range surrounding the mobile base station. Callers within this cell will communicate via the base station.

The service provider deploys base stations, and thus cells, throughout the coverage area. Two people having a wireless conversation in different cells will communicate via their local base stations. These in turn will communicate with each other to ensure the link is made between the two callers.

The cellular approach is sophisticated as it enables the service provider to maximise the number of customers using the service. A non-cellular approach would require one giant base station. This would:

- ❑ Have limited geographical coverage
- ❑ Result in a reduced maximum number of concurrent users
- ❑ Fry those that lived close by.

One of the challenges of cellular technology is how to handle the situation where the caller moves from one cell to another.

What's radio got to do with it? Radio is a reference to the fact that this form of wireless communications uses the 'radio part' of the electromagnetic spectrum, much like actual radios. It does not imply that your radio could double up as a mobile phone, but it does imply they use similar communication technology.

Today it is solved, but in the recent past 'dropped calls' resulting from the caller moving into a cell with no available channels was quite common.

It is also quite common for people to talk about first, second and third generation mobile technology. I have not encountered universal agreement on 1st and 2nd generation, but it wouldn't be far wrong to suggest that the former offered voice services only, ie. calls and voice mail, whilst the second offered voice plus data related services, for example SMS (Short Messaging Service aka texting) and rudimentary access to the WWW (Wap in the UK comes to mind).

The telecoms marketing departments did a lot of damage to the credibility of the wireless industry. Users familiar with accessing the Internet via the desktop were very under whelmed by the poor navigation and interface offered by Wap. Despite these shortcomings it underpins the bulk of wireless financial transactions in the world today.

We are currently waiting for 3G (third generation) mobile services. Again the promise of 3G has been pushed for several years now and it is yet to arrive in a groundbreaking manner.

3G is essentially broadband (video quality content) to the palm. This includes the ability to watch video via one's mobile phone or PDA. Today we have pseudo 3G, which some refer to as 2½G, which allows you to watch video clips and send photographs. But this is some way off true 3G.

The promise of 3G will include:

- ❑ Faster downloads
- ❑ Video quality content
- ❑ Enhanced experience – more intuitive.

As mentioned earlier in this chapter the use of head up displays and foldable screens will eliminate the limitations of the phone/PDA screens.

Again the issue of combining voice and data services onto one machine seems questionable. Hands-free listening devices will enable people that call you to see your face rather than your inner ear.

Please note that the acquiring of a 3G licence was a costly affair. Within Europe circa £100bn was generated for the governments concerned. At the time it seemed a good idea in the way that having an oxygen licence might seem good today, what with oxygen being so popular with humans.

The auctions coincided with the dotcom hubris and so the service providers saw the issue of payback as a detail. They are desperately awaiting the 'killer application' that will have consumers / businesses willing to pay large sums for 3G services.

In the absence of the killer app, some of the operators have reverted to more traditional and seedier approaches to extracting money, ie. pornography. Certain companies will carry this off as 'fun/lifestyle' in the same way that for example Cosmopolitan magazine makes raunchiness part of their brand. Some may just as well redesign their logo around a dirty raincoat motif.

The business point is that sex sells and the operators are desperate for payback. Clearly images and video lend themselves to this type of content. But plans to turn the mobile phone into a 'virtual girlfriend' ('Tamagotchi'?) device are at the very least enterprising. The associated accessory catalogues of mobile phone operators may eventually require censor control.

One of the emerging technology driven themes of the last few years is e-learning. It is proving to be as successful as computer-based training, ie not very. However I do feel it offers real potential when teamed up with 3G to offer tactical 'just-in-time' modular training when and where the recipient requires it.

Roadside mechanics encountering an unfamiliar car can download the appropriate tutorial. A business developer who is just about to meet an absent colleague's client can download a corporate summary and swot up in the waiting room prior to the meeting.

Whilst entertainment looks to be the way forward for cellular, I think there is a real business opportunity in the knowledge management domain.

Non cellular radio

As the vendors raced to acquire 3G licences, two technologies were quietly making their way to the fore. These technologies were focused on wireless communication but only over a relatively short distance (10 – 100 metres).

The technologies in question are Bluetooth and Wi-Fi (aka 802.11b, 802.11h etc and WLAN). To be more accurate these are specifications from which technologies are built. Most importantly a government licence is not required to deploy the service.

Bluetooth

Bluetooth is geared towards machine-to-machine communication. Think wireless hands-free mobile phone. This has great potential. Think of a future where your alarm clock triggers the shower and coffee percolator to activate. Or a fridge that recognizes that you are low on milk and places an order for more online (having negotiated the best deal). Or even bathroom furniture suppliers who team up with health care providers to offer real-time health monitoring. You join up the dots on this one.

Bluetooth being short range will enable the appropriate appliance to communicate with the domestic server (every home will have one, even if it is Microsoft's X-box), which in turn will handle the Internet communication in the usual manner.

In the medium term this will be a great cause for neighbour-related disputes. Once the security is properly resolved it will be less likely that your alarm will scare the life out of the neighbours by inadvertently turning their shower on.

Wi-Fi

Wi-Fi (Wireless Fidelity, a play on Hi-Fi) is a relative newcomer. Some would say that it has overtaken Bluetooth as a short-range wireless communication approach. The reality is that their strengths are different. Wi-Fi is much more like traditional local area networking, hence the alternative sobriquet WLAN (Wireless Local Area Network).

Thus it offers a wire free office environment, making it possible for cool techie entrepreneurs to set up shop in castles and other environments that traditionally don't come with raised flooring or cable ducts.

With the convergence of voice and data onto the one network, Wi-Fi phones will become increasingly popular. Particularly ones that flit from Wi-Fi to cellular based on location.

Unlike 3G these non-cellular technologies are on the ascendancy. If you think about it, the bulk of the population, in Western countries at least, are to be found in what are known as 'hotspots', for example hotels, schools, business parks, airports, railways stations, Starbucks, McDonalds and so on. Thus we now have a solution that addresses the needs of the majority of the users and doesn't require a multi-billion pound licence.

So in one fell swoop the need for 3G is obviated. The lesson here is that the longer the period between acquiring and deploying a technology, the more likely an interim technology will creep in and ruin your plans.

One of the few technology growth games in town at the time of writing is the race to wirelessly wire up these 'hotspots'.

Impact on business

The integration of knowledge management with cellular technologies will give staff the benefits of being in the office when out in the field.

Wire free offices with integrated telephony will become the norm. Unless there is some form of employee backlash, employers will be able to check up on where the staff are, not by surreptitious triangulation techniques, but simply by observing the backdrop of the possibly errant employee when 'speaking' over the phone. There clearly is an opportunity here for developing backdrop wallpaper technology that eg. provides the setting of a train, for use when your partner is expecting you home and you are in fact out on the town.

Impact on the IT department

This will place a great burden on IT departments. It's like laptops only worse from a security perspective. Though the use of a thin-client architect (see chapter 6) could mitigate against this.

Impact on consumers

There is a question mark over whether consumers want or even need more technology in their palm. Is there really a market for integrated phone and camera? The use of such phones to steal content from newsagents, by 'snapping' the pages of the article of interest, without the burden of paying for the magazine, is a practical albeit illegal use of this technology.

Look out for suspicious characters wearing raincoats and glasses. That peculiar grin accompanying the suspicious pocket action could well be someone rewinding a comedy video delivered via the airport's wireless network using their mobile phone as the controller and the glasses as the display.

Artificial Intelligence

Overview

Also known as AI, artificial intelligence is a generic term that describes man's attempts to replicate the manner in which our brains function in order to carry out specific tasks. Type 'what is neuroscience' into Google if you need more detail.

Many of these tasks come surprisingly easy to humans, for example extracting a car registration number from a speed camera photograph, but it is a real challenge for a computer.

In broad terms AI has been a disappointment, but its future looks both promising and scary. Given that rate of technological innovation, AI should have already delivered robotic butlers and chambermaids. But the simple act of climbing stairs or negotiating doors is an extremely difficult challenge for a computer today. Please note that I am not referring to a computer in the sense of a laptop or server, but one with 'limbs' and the ability to process sensory information, eg. the ability to see and act on what it sees.

Having got that frustration off my chest, progress has been made, so we will take a look at some of the major developments that will likely form part of our future.

Biometrics

Security is not only a basic human need, it is a very topical one given the world we now live in. Privacy today extends to more than 'net curtains' (surely a great name for a privacy product) now that identity theft is a reality.

We touched on biometrics in Chapter 10. The theme here is to use 'what you are' as a means of authentication. Options include:

- ❑ Fingerprint
- ❑ Voice
- ❑ Cranium
- ❑ Face.

Many people claim to never forget a face. But very few can be so confident when it comes to fingerprints. A face, for example, is recorded and then mathematically dissected to reduce what was essentially a picture into a set of parameter values, eg. distance between eyes. The AI bit is in determining whether a person subsequently claiming to own that face is indeed that person. A change in hairstyle, a beard, chicken pox, anaphylactic attacks all conspire to undermine the matching. The AI technology using perhaps statistical analysis will take a view on whether there is a match. Again even with the best-trained airport security staff it would be something of a burden to expect them to remember the faces of all known terrorists, football hooligans and heads of state.

Expert Systems

Medicine, law and any other rote learning based professions need to be giving some thought to the 'value-add' element of their role, once expert systems kick in. Essentially such systems can store the static information that underpins their expertise, such as the leg bone's connected to the foot bone....

248

Either with the help of a professional representative or by recording their outputs based on given inputs the expert system can 'learn' how to respond on future occasions. Unlike 'time starved' lawyers, the expert system can keep up to date with changes in the law and scan all cases ever tried in a very short period of time when looking for precedents.

Case-based reasoning is a halfway house to full expert systems. Here the system looks at what outputs (treatments) are associated with the given inputs (symptoms). Such systems are useful, but in a limited way. True expert systems will develop a 'gut feeling' for situations where they do not have a previous case to fall back on.

IBM and the other box shifters are getting into Business Process Outsourcing (BPO), where they effectively take charge of the operational aspects of the Finance or HR departments. It is just a matter of time before IBM will be approaching the law firms with a compelling vision.

Robotics

As mentioned we are some way off mistaking androids for humans. A simple act such as handshaking is a great challenge for an android. The level of pressure needs to lie somewhere between 'bone crushing' and limp.

In the commercial world robots are utilized in factory automation. But their potential in relieving people of the tedium of life, eg. tidying up the house, assembling fiddly components in a factory, gardening (for Type A personalities) is significant.

Relieving people of the more risky aspects of life, eg. policing (that gives me an idea for a film) might also have value. The roles of navy seal, traffic warden, roofing specialist and teacher may also benefit.

Worryingly this far-reaching element of a postindustrial society is underpinned by fiction. Though having said that it is true of most innovations. So we can conclude that our ability to innovate is only limited by our ability to dream.

Consequently much of robotic science is underpinned by the fictional writings of author Isaac Asimov. Specifically his robot laws, which follow:

- ❑ A robot may not injure a human being, or, through inaction, allow a human being to come to harm

- A robot must obey the orders given it by human beings except where such orders would conflict with the First Law
- A robot must protect its own existence as long as such protection does not conflict with the First or Second Law.

There is also a zeroth law, which was created to patch over the shortcoming of the three laws above:

- A robot may not injure humanity, or, through inaction, allow humanity to come to harm.

So if a robot is on a mission to save the world, does that empower it to kill individuals to ensure humanity is saved? I personally would like someone to spend a little bit of time thinking these through before robotics becomes too mainstream.

For robots to become as 'sophisticated' as humans there will need to be great strides taken in human neurosystem replication.

We are starting to see that it may be easier to harness the human neurosystem and replace less robust elements of the human with bionic components. There is at least one example of a UK academic that has successfully grafted silicon to human tissue and is now able to hook himself up to electronic devices. This gives me an idea for what could well be a successful TV series.

NB. The work carried out by the cyborg academic has far reaching consequences. He and others have proven the concept of thought driven computers. This will be a boon to those who do not have control of their limbs, eg quadriplegics, or those who do not have use to their limbs, for example a fireman hanging from a beam in a burning building who needs to get out fast but needs to manipulate the building plans displayed onto his helmet visor.

Impact on business

Human resources will be intrigued by the possibilities here. If your colleague's voice sounds different, or they walk slightly differently after an appraisal, its safe to say you have been working with a cyborg. It will add a whole new meaning to the term HR toolkit.

Impact on the IT department

I suspect that robot related issues would in the first instance be dealt with by HR. If they cannot handle it there will no doubt be a relationship already in place with a biotech supplier. Watch the R&D spend of the major biotech companies over the next few years.

Impact on consumers

If robots do advance to human-like levels, then the impact on us will be profound.

Smart clothing

Overview

It would be easy to make facetious comments such as this is an area that has been ignored by the IT community. But what I am really getting at is the integration of clothing with IT.

14.4 The next step in smart clothing?

I was an early adopter. My school shoes had a compass built into the sole. My parents should have seen the early warning signs. Though I suppose it would have been more worrying if it were I rather than the shoe manufacturer that handled the integration.

In latter years coats have encompassed clocks/stop watches and more recently MP3 players.

But truly smart clothing is much more sophisticated and will be with us sooner rather than later.

Military application

Your soldiers are behind enemy lines. The radio signals suggest that they are under heavy fire. You can pin point the location of each soldier through wireless technology built into their clothing.

The question is do you risk sending in a helicopter to rescue them? You check the screen, soldier one has been shot in the leg, but it is a graze. You check to ensure the clothing has released antiseptic and painkillers as it is programmed to do when the suit is penetrated.

Soldier two has taken a shot to the head his vital signals are 'flat lining'.

You alert soldier three, who appears to be in good health, other than his pulse being dangerously high, that soldier two is dead, but that soldier one needs to be pulled out of the line of fire. The exact location of a safe cover is mapped onto soldier three's infrared goggles.

Welcome to digital war. No more heroics, it's all about data processing and analysis.

Civilian application

Essentially a less dramatic scenario. The life insurance company sees the patient as high risk, but insurable. A condition of getting insurance is that the insured must wear the smart vest. This monitors and communicates all vital signals. If certain data trends emerge the insurance company can mandate treatment. If certain one off events occur, for example the insured's temperature drops below a pre-defined threshold, the hospital will be notified immediately and the emergency services will be actioned.

Welcome to digital wellness.

Social application

You are late for a first date. In your haste to catch the train you trip and submerge your knee in a murky puddle. You are stressed and getting increasingly overheated and sweaty by the second.

Fortunately you are wearing smart fibre clothing. As you sit there thinking of things to say on the date that will imply that you are cultured, passionate yet capable of deferred gratification, your trousers are effecting a self-clean using the latest microbe technology. Also your clothing has automatically released air vents to allow a conduit of air to pass through your clothing and thereby bring you back to normal temperature.

The final touch is the options you have with respect to scenting, Gucci or Calvin Klein? This may be limited to the offerings of the clothing manufacturer.

Welcome to digital dating.

Impact on business

Little impact, unless you are in the clothing business. Might be useful where your staff spend a lot of time away from the office. At one level you can keep track of them. If micromanagement (or even nano-management) has appeal you could also ascertain whether they are genuinely sick and apply appropriate medication remotely.

Impact on the IT department

There may be a need to create policy around digital clothing, as it may represent a technology security risk and may interfere with the wireless office network.

Impact on consumers

We will no doubt wonder how we survived without smart clothing at some point, particularly from a health perspective. There may well be privacy issues to address. Bored techies may have fun by remotely activating inappropriate functions by overriding the inbuilt security features of their line manager's clothing.

Social Consequences

Even though much of what we have covered lends itself to light-hearted observations, there are real social implications in rushing down the technology innovation road.

Dumping technology into an organization in the vague hope that it will increase profitability will always end in failure. Technology deployment impacts people and processes. Ignore the impact and failure will be guaranteed.

Much of the technology innovation is taking place because vendors see it as a way to make money. Their in-house experts see technology innovation as an intellectual exercise.

These organizations do not always care about the social impact, other than how to exploit social behaviour for marketing purposes.

As mentioned in an earlier chapter, society is likely to spawn a digital divide, whereby the disadvantaged slip further behind as technology enables those better off to increasingly have a Utopian existence.

This schism is well underway. There are some people today who have well paid jobs and are counting their lucky stars. They are oblivious to the fact that they will in fact join the disadvantaged if they do not re-skill fast.

There is a pressure on businesses to be more efficient. Thus in time if a computer can do your job it will. Sitting at your PC thinking you are a knowledge worker and therefore on the winning side in what is the information revolution (read up on the agricultural and industrial revolutions for more details) might be misguided. The secret is to provide a service that cannot be delivered using computers alone. As mentioned, even doctors and lawyers need to rethink their career plans, as knowledge-based computing becomes a reality.

More positively it will provide many people with a lot more free time. One scenario is that computers will do all the work and humans will be able to wile away the years pursuing 'higher endeavours'.

On a less positive note, people may become disillusioned as their primal urges to hunt and gather become unnecessary. Thousands of years of genetic programming, which latterly we have adapted to work (hunt) and shop (gather), will be thwarted. The consequences of that do not bear thinking about.

Thus society needs to carefully manage the deployment and utilisation of technology rather than let this be dictated by technology vendors.

Perhaps this is more an issue for our descendents, but the seeds are being sown today.

In summary

- ❑ Whilst the technology we use today appears smart, it is primitive compared to its potential
- ❑ Once artificial intelligence techniques become standard we will see a quantum leap in terms of capability
- ❑ Computing will cease to be an activity that requires a desktop computer. The TV, the wristwatch and even the bathroom cabinet will all become communication/information access points
- ❑ The acceleration of technology adoption could well have negative social implications, and so must be managed.

Test yourself?

49. Comparative shopping:

    a. Relies on having common data labelling standards

    b. Will enable you to compare your purchases with other net shoppers

    c. Will put the merchants at a great advantage over consumers

    d. Will work best when procuring commodities.

50. Interactive TV:

    a. Is a serious threat to those that prefer passive entertainment

    b. Will enable designer programming

    c. Has some privacy issues

    d. Will enable advertisers to be more focused in targeting their market.

51. KM:

    a. Is a term used to describe the harnessing of what people know in an organization

    b. Is key to helping organizations learn from their mistakes

    c. Underpins the test taken by London taxi drivers

    d. Is the death of classroom based training.

52. Nano-technology:

    a. Will enable parents to send salvage submarines into their children's bodies to retrieve swallowed coins and other nutrition-free objects

    b. Was pioneered by US scientists Mork and Mindy

    c. Has great potential in healthcare

    d. Was originally designed to replicate grandmothers.

53. Smart clothing:

    a. Will enable you to eliminate embarrassment caused by other people attending the same social function as you wearing the same outfit

    b. Will have health monitoring functionality

    c. Will enable health insurance companies/battlefield commanders to establish whether you are 'beyond economic repair'

    d. Will very likely have Internet access.

Index

Index

Index

Index

About Auridian

About Auridian

Cost management, competitive advantage and governance are all strategically good reasons to invest in IT. Auridian helps organisations extract maximum value from their IT investment.

We believe that people are the key to this. Our clients range from the world's largest banks to start-up IT recruitment consultancies. We work with board level executives through to new entrant technologists.

Clients value:

- Our ability to demystify new technology terminology

- Our view on new technology market trends

- Our understanding of how new technologies impact business.

Visit **www.auridian.com** for more details.

Promotional

IT Demystified – The Seminar

We hope that you have found this book to be of value. Why not test-drive our IT Demystified seminar? Call us now on +44 (0) 1494 866 799 or email us at info@auridian.com to book your place (plus that of a colleague if you like) at our favourable 'test-drive' rate.

You have now read the book, so why not attend the theatre production?!

For more details visit:

www.auridian.com